Social influence

SNAPREVISE

Explanations of conformity

- **Compliance:** to conform with the majority publicly for acceptance or approval whilst **disagreeing privately**. Our adopted opinions only last as long as we are with the majority group.
- **Internalisation:** a type of conformity where we take on the views and attitudes of the majority group because we agree that they are correct. We **agree both publicly and privately.**
- **Normative social influence:** occurs when an individual conforms to norms of the majority even if they privately disagree. This is because as humans we have a **biological fear of rejection** and a fundamental need for social approval. The need to 'fit in' to avoid being viewed as an 'outcast' is an **emotional response.**
- **Informational social influence:** occurs when an individual conforms because they are unsure in a situation. We look to others who we believe are more certain of the situation to guide us. This explanation of conformity is driven by a **biological need to be right** and is a **cognitive response.**

Evaluating conformity

◆ **Asch's (1951)** *study provides evidence for both normative and informational social influence. The conformity rates increasing in the task difficulty variation show evidence for informational social influence as when people were unsure of the correct answer, they looked for someone they thought were correct to follow. Additionally, it shows evidence for normative social influence as even though people knew the correct answers, they still followed the majority group for fear of not 'fitting in.'*

◆ **Lucas et. al. (2006)** *conducted a study using students and maths tests of varying difficulty. He asked students to give answers to maths questions that were either hard or easy. He found that there was a higher conformity rate for difficult questions than easy ones. This supports informational social influence as it shows that there are higher rates of conformity where people are unsure of their knowledge and not confident in their abilities.*

◆ ***Cultural bias:*** *historically, most conformity research took place in individualist cultures. Evidence has shown that in collectivist cultures, such as China, conformity rates are often higher. For example,* **Smith and Bond (1996)** *found higher conformity rates in Japan, which shows that most research into conformity may not be generalisable across cultures.*

Asch's research into conformity

- **Aim:** Asch conducted a lab experiment which examined c… ich people will conform to the opinion of others, even in a situation where the answe…
- **Participants:** 123 male American college students; each participant took part in 18 trials. In the first four, the confederates gave the correct answers, and then slowly started to give incorrect ones. The next 12 trials were called the critical trials where all of the confederates gave incorrect answers.
- **Method:** Asch created an artificial environment where people believed they were taking part in a vision test. He asked the students to make judgements on a simple line task and ask to compare them to a line marked 'X'. Asch had set up the room with seven confederates and only one naïve participant. The confederates had been told to purposely answer the task incorrectly. This was to test whether it would influence the naïve participant to conform. He ensured that the naïve participant was sat last or second to last to guarantee that the naïve participant had heard the confederates' answers first.

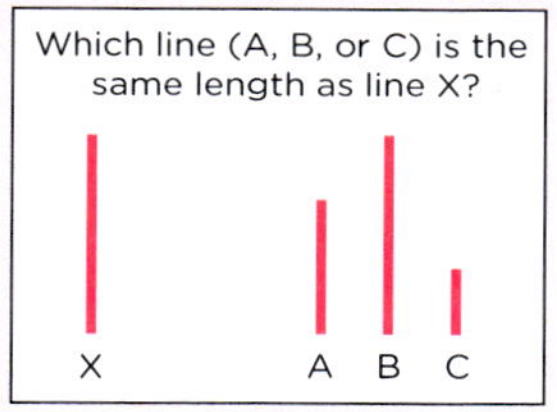

- **Results:** 75% of people conformed at least once. The overall conformity rate was at 37%. When there was no unanimity, the conformity rate dropped to 5%.
- **Variations:** Asch and subsequent researchers also investigated the conditions that affect conformity rates, including:
  - **Group size:** with a group of three, the conformity rate grew to 31%. When he increased the number, there was an insignificant increase in conformity rate – 37% was the highest when in a group of 7. He concluded that only 3 people are needed for conformity to take place.
  - **Task difficulty:** if the task is more difficult, the conformity rate increases. This is because when people are unsure in a situation, they look to others for the correct answer. Therefore, when the task is easier, people are less likely to be influenced by others.
  - **Unanimity:** in a variation, a confederate was told to give correct answers. When another person gave correct answers, the conformity rate dropped to around 5%. Therefore, if unanimity is broken, the rate of conformity is reduced.
- Evaluation:
  - ◆ ***Highly controlled study:*** *lab experiments have high internal validity, so Asch's results wouldn't be affected by extraneous variables.*
  - ◆ ***Cultural bias:*** *may only have produced these findings because of the context of the time. It was conducted in 1950s America during the Cold War where being seen as the 'odd one out' was dangerous. Conformity and solidarity was seen as the norm in society and any deviation from these views was viewed as 'un-American.' Therefore, results may not be generalisable across time periods and cultures.*
  - ◆ ***Only used males:*** *the results are not generalisable to women or fully representative of the population.*
  - ◆ ***Ethical issues:*** *Asch's study used deception as the participants were led to believe that they were in a room of naïve participants when they were actually confederates. Another ethical issue is psychological distress, as the naïve participants were led to believe that an obvious correct answer was incorrect. This may have led to stress and confusion.*

Dispositional explanation for obedience

- **Adorno (1947)** believed blind obedience was the result of a dispositional factor. He wanted to investigate whether there was a specific personality type who were more likely to accept authority. He created a questionnaire called the 'F-scale' and handed it to over 2000 middle class Americans. Those who scored highly on the F-scale: had more of a contemptuous view of those who were 'vulnerable' or 'weak' in society, were conscious of their own status, believed those of higher authority were more deserving of respect, had high levels of prejudice, and were overall heavily submissive to authority.
- Adorno also theorised that this personality type originated in childhood as a result of harsh, loveless parenting where they were only shown conditional love when doing something good. They were raised strictly with a high expectation of loyalty regardless of the treatment towards them.

Resistance to social influence

- There are dispositional and situational factors that encourage us to withstand social pressures to obey.
- **Social support:** is a situational factor because when people agree with you in a situation, it is easier to resist the pressure to conform. This was explored in Asch's variations where he showed that with social support, conformity rates rapidly decrease. If someone agrees with us, it gives us confidence to speak out.
- **Locus of control (LOC): Rotter (1966)** examined the sense of control people believe they have over their own lives. Locus of control refers to the control that external or internal forces have over events in their lives. He believed that everyone can be placed on a scale: you can lie on the eternal LOC end or the internal LOC end. He tested this by using a questionnaire. He found that people with a high internal LOC are more likely to resist social pressures as they accept more responsibility for their actions, so are unlikely to look to authority for guidance. They are active seekers of information and generally regarded as more intelligent. They are also achievement oriented based on their own expectations which gives them less of a need for social approval.

Minority influence

- **Moscovici (1969)** theorised that minority groups can also exert pressure on majority groups; it's not just the other way around. He set up an experiment with 6 people and showed them blue coloured slides and then asked if they were blue or green. There were two confederates who consistently and then inconsistently said the slides were green. When both said green, the agreement rate was 8%. However, when they inconsistently agreed, the agreement rate dropped to 1%. From this research, he concluded that in order for a minority group to have an influence on a majority group, there needed to be consistency, commitment, and flexibility.
  - **Consistency:** can be **synchronic** (where everyone says the same thing) or **diachronic** (where they continue to say the same thing over time).
  - **Commitment:** it's more difficult to dismiss a minority group when they show a great level of commitment to their principles – especially when they compromise their own safety for the cause. Commitment involving a loss like disapproval from the majority is more likely to gain attention and convince the majority to take them seriously.

Milgram's study into obedience

- **Aim: Milgram (1961)** wanted to understand why Nazi soldiers in WWII were so obedient. It was assumed that German soldiers were less moral than Americans and that is why they obeyed commands so willingly (i.e. more dispositional factors than situational factors). Milgram wanted to test this in a lab experiment at Yale university.
- **Participants:** the experiment was conducted with 40 males using volunteer sampling (an advert in the newspaper and leaflets).
- **Method:** a naïve participant was the 'teacher' who tested the learner with basic questions. The 'learner' and the 'experimenter' were both confederates. The learner was attached to electrodes which would 'shock' him for a wrong answer. The naïve participant was told that the study was about how punishment can improve memory, but the true aim was to test whether a person would obey an authority figure by electrocuting a stranger.
- **Results:** participants showed signs of stress when eliciting the shocks but still followed through. All participants shocked up to 300V after hearing the learner scream. 65% of participants shocked to the maximum of 450V.
- **Conclusion:** Milgram disproved the dispositional factor.

Obedience: situational variables

- Milgram wanted to explain why we surrender our independence to authority figures so easily. He argued that from early childhood we are taught to respect authority and that in a given context, certain people have 'legitimate authority.' This begins with respecting our parents and teachers in childhood and then develops into respecting institutions like the police. We trust these figures to exert their power responsibly.
- Milgram repeated this experiment with different variables to explore whether it would change the levels of obedience. This included:
  - **Uniform:** he changed the lab coat and clipboard of the experimenter to a casual t-shirt and jeans. This decreased the perceived authority of the experimenter and their academic importance.
  - **Location:** moved from Yale University to a run-down, downtown office.
  - **Proximity:** moving teacher to the same room as the learner, or even telling them to force the learner's hand onto the shock plate allowed them to see the consequences of their actions. He also did trials with the experimenter in another room.
  - **Social support:** two additional confederates in the room refused to shock the learner.
- Obedience dropped to: **10%** when social support refused to shock the learner, **20%** when the experimenter was in casual clothing, **20.5%** when the experimenter left the room, **30%** when the teacher forces hand on the shock plate, and **48%** in a downtown office.
- **Agentic shift:** when person with perceived authority gives someone an order, they go through a shift from an autonomous state (where people direct their own behaviour and take responsibility for their actions) to an agentic state (where people act by the orders of a perceived authority and believe that the responsibility for their actions can be attributed to the person giving the order).
- **Binding factors:** Milgram argued that even when participants knew that their behaviour was causing harm and were acting in ways against their morality, they continued due to things called binding factors. These include factors such as politeness, the desire to uphold a promise of helping, and fear of awkwardness if they withdraw from the experiment.

The multi-store memory model

- **Features of memory:**
  - **Capacity:** the amount of information that can be held in a memory store.
  - **Duration:** the length of time information can be held in our brains.
  - **Coding:** how we process the information.
- **The multi-store memory model:**
  - Created by **Atkinson and Shiffrin (1968)** to describe how information flows through the memory system.
  - The model is structured with three separate stores and linear information flow.

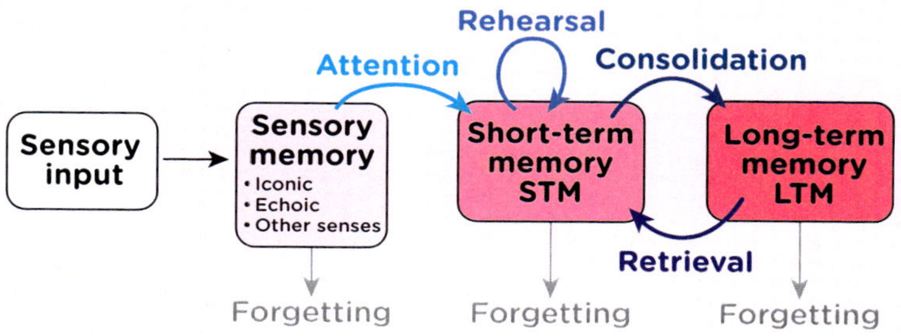

- **Features of the stores:**
  - **Short term memory (STM):** the duration is between 18–30 seconds unless it is rehearsed. It has limited capacity (7 ± 2 items) and information in this store is coded acoustically.
  - **Long term memory (LTM):** the duration is partially permanent when information has been rehearsed. The capacity is seemingly unlimited and the information is coded semantically.
  - **Sensory register:** the duration is less than a second. It has a very large capacity and it codes echoic and iconically. A stimulus from the environment passes into the sensory register. The sensory register gathers its information from the environment. Most of the information receives no attention. Only information that has attention paid to it will pass to the short-term memory. The sensory register has five stores (one for each of the senses) but the main ones are the echoic and iconic stores:
    - **Echoic:** auditory information, coded acoustically.
    - **Iconic:** visual information, coded visually.
  - **Maintenance rehearsal:** this is where we repeat information to ourselves. It increases the amount of time that information will be held in the STM. If it is done for long enough, the information will pass into the LTM.
  - **Retrieval:** when information is recalled from the LTM to the STM.
- Evaluation of the multi-store memory model:
  - ◆ ***Wilson, Kopelman, and Kapur (2008)** studied a musician named Clive Wearing who contracted a brain infection that left him with a memory span of less than 30 seconds. However, his musical ability remained intact. This supports the multi-store memory model as it shows there are different stores for memory (i.e. he has LTM but no STM).*
  - ◆ ***Shallice and Warrington (1974)** studied a brain-damaged patient KF whose short-term memory was severely compromised, only being able to remember 2 items instead of the average 7. When it was tested visually, it was close to normal, but when testing in an auditory way, he had bad recall. This criticises the multi-store memory model as it suggests that there has to be more than one STM.*

The working memory model

- This model was proposed by **Baddeley and Hitch (1974)**. It describes the STM as a system with multiple components. These include:
  - **Central executive:** decides what working memory pays attention to. It has limited capacity but can code any type of information. It is like a manager in that it gives tasks to the other systems depending on whether it is visual or auditory, monitoring them and taking over when necessary. However, a task that requires a lot of attention or is new will overload it.
  - **Phonological loop:** auditory information is passed on from the central executive to the phonological loop. It is divided into two sections – the phonological store (which stores words we hear) and the articulatory loop (which silently rehearses words that we have seen or heard to keep them in our memory). It has limited capacity and it codes acoustically.
  - **The visuospatial sketch pad:** visual and spatial information is passed from the central executive to the VSS which is used to plan spatial tasks and set mental images. It has a limited capacity and codes visually.
  - **The episodic buffer:** this element was added into the model added later by **Baddeley and Hitch (2000)** when they realised the original model did not account for storage. The episodic buffer collects and merges information from the other stores in order to record an event. It transfers information and retrieves information from the LTM to the STM. It has a limited capacity and can code any type of information.
- Evaluation of the working memory model:
  - ◆ *In **Shallice and Warrington's (1974)** case study of KF who suffered from a severe brain injury and had bad STM for verbal information, they found he could process visual information. This shows support for the model as it gives evidence for there being multiple stores within STM, such as the visuospatial sketchpad and the phonological loop.*
  - ◆ *This model was produced based on evidence from lab experiments which makes the results reliable as they can easily be replicated. It also means there is likely to be confounding variables affecting the studies.*
  - ◆ *The central executive is argued to be a single component that delegates roles to different systems. However, some psychologists argue that there may be different stores within the central executive function, so there isn't a consensus around this component or the model as a whole.*

SNAPREVISE

Explanations for forgetting

- **Interference theory:**
  - Interference occurs when two pieces of information conflict with one another which may result in forgetting one or both pieces of information, or distortion of memory. This explanation of forgetting is usually associated with LTM where information is theoretically permanent but harder to access, which makes forgetting more likely.
  - According to this theory, forgetting is when interference makes it harder to locate a memory. Information in the LTM can also be disrupted by other information during coding, which leads to inaccurate recall.
  - Two types of interference:
    - **Proactive interference:** when previously stored information interferes with the attempt to recall newly added information.
    - **Retroactive interference:** when new information interferes with the attempt to recall previously stored information.
  - Evaluation of interference theory
    - ◆ **McGeoch and McDonald (1931)** *conducted research into the 'effects of similarity' using a lab study. They gave participants a list of ten words, waited ten minutes, and then gave them another list of ten words that were different from the first list. They asked participants to recall the original list of words and found that many couldn't. They concluded that retroactive interference had occurred as the newest information had interfered with the old. This shows evidence for interference as an explanation for forgetting.*
    - ◆ **Baddeley and Hitch (1977)** *used a natural experiment to test the 'effects of similarity' in recall. They asked a group of rugby players to list the names of previous teams they had played against. Some players had played in all the games whereas others had only played in a few. They discovered that players who had played in all the games forgot proportionally more teams than those who had only played in some. They concluded that the forgetting therefore wasn't due to the amount of time passed between games but rather the games getting confused in memory due to a larger amount of unfamiliar information. This shows support for interference theory.*
- **Retrieval failure:** forgetting occurs when information is in the LTM but cannot be accessed due to an absence of memory cues. Memory cues can be meaningful or accidental. Accidental cues fall into two categories:
  - **Context-dependent forgetting:** occurs due to a lack of external retrieval cues. When the external environment differs from the one that we were in during encoding, there are no external retrieval cues to trigger remembering. For example, if you complete a test in the same classroom you learnt the information, you're more likely to remember it than if the test is in another room.
  - **State-dependent forgetting:** occurs due to a lack of internal memory cues. When an individual's internal state is different from how it was during encoding, there are no internal retrieval cues to trigger remembering. For example, completing a class test when anxious would be less effective than when relaxed if you were relaxed when learning the information.

Factors affecting the accuracy of eye-witness testimony

- **Leading questions:** are question that are phrased in a way that suggests or guides the respondent towards a particular answer rather than allowing for an unbiased response. A leading question can alter or distort memory recall by introducing information that may not have originally been present, demonstrating that memory is not a perfect recording, but can be influenced, reconstructed, or even contaminated by suggestion.
  - **Loftus and Palmer (1974)** investigated the impact of question phrasing on eye-witness testimony. They conducted a lab experiment with 45 American students. They were shown a video of a car crash and asked the question 'How fast were the cars travelling when they ______ each other?' with variations of the term 'crashed' (i.e. smashed, hit, collided, bumped, or contacted). They discovered that when students were asked the question with the verb 'smashed,' they guessed a higher mean speed than those who were asked with the verb 'contacted.' They concluded that the phrasing of a question can influence a participant's memory of an event.
  - Evaluation of leading questions:
    - ◆ *Practical application: this research helped to reform police questioning techniques and discourage the use of leading questions – instead they use cognitive interview techniques to prevent wrongful convictions.*
    - ◆ *Internal validity: this was a lab experiment so had high internal validity as it took place in a highly controlled environment. They had control over extraneous variables and could establish a cause and effect.*
    - ◆ *External validity: because the lab is an artificial environment, there was no emotional impact or consequence over answer given, so results may not be generalisable to the real world.*

Factors affecting the accuracy of eye-witness testimony (continued)

- **Post-event discussion:** when witnesses of a crime discuss the event with one another, their eye-witness testimony can become distorted as they combine misinformation from other witnesses with their own memory.
  - **Gabbert et al. (2003)** conducted a lab experiment showing a video of a girl stealing money from a wallet. The participants were either tested in peers (co-witnesses) or individually. The participants were told they were watching the same video, but they were from different perspectives. The co-witness groups discussed the event afterwards whereas the individual (control) group didn't. They discovered that 71% of the co-witness group mistakenly recalled information they had not seen. In the control group without discussion, the figure of misinformation was 0%. They concluded that post-event discussion can affect a person's memory of an event and that witnesses will go along with each other.
  - Evaluation of post-event discussion:
    - *Practical application: this informs the legal system and practice of discouraging jurors from discussing the case outside of the courtroom.*
    - *Internal validity: this was a lab experiment so was highly controlled and standardised, establishing cause and effect.*
    - *External validity: a lab experiment doesn't reflect real world eye-witness testimony.*
- **Anxiety:** has strong emotional and physical effects on a person, but it's unclear whether it has a positive or negative effect on recall of eye-witness testimony.
  - **Positive effect:** **Christianson and Hubinette (1993)** investigated if anxiety increases or decreases the accuracy of eyewitness testimony. They interviewed 58 real victims of a bank robbery. These people were either directly threatened or just witnesses. They discovered that those who had been directly threatened had significantly better memories of the event than the witnesses. They concluded therefore that anxiety increases the accuracy of eyewitness testimony.
  - **Negative effect:** **Johnson and Scott (1976)** investigated the effects of anxiety in the accuracy of eyewitness testimony using a lab experiment. Participants were placed in one of two conditions where a person was carrying something intended to provoke high anxiety (weapon), or low anxiety (pen). They then had to identify the person who left the room from fifty photographs. They discovered a 49% accuracy rate in the low anxiety condition as opposed to 33% in the high anxiety condition. They concluded that anxiety caused weapon-focus as the witness only concentrated on the weapon and not the person.
  - **Yerkes Dodson Law:** is a principle that peak task performance comes at an intermediate level of stress. Too much or too little stress will cause a drop in performance. Therefore, an intermediate level of anxiety could be argued to be optimal for accuracy of eye-witness testimony.
    - *Harm: these investigations into the effect of anxiety on accuracy of eye-witness testimony may have caused psychological harm to their participants which breaks ethical research guidelines.*
    - *Low external validity: lab experiments are harder to generalise to real world situations. In a real, high anxiety, situation, people may act differently due to shock or the fact that there may be consequences of their testimony.*
- **The cognitive interview:** developed by **Fisher et al (1990)**, who watched real police interviews and concluded that there were issues with the standard interview. Cognitive interviews had open-ended questions, did not interrupt participants, and thus had more retrieval paths. Standard interviews had closed, direct questions, often interrupted participants, and thus had fewer retrieval paths.
  - **Fisher and Geiselman (1992)** developed the cognitive interview which is a technique used by police to interview witnesses after they've seen a crime or accident to help facilitate the most accurate and detailed memory possible.
  - Features of the cognitive interview:
    - **Recall everything:** report all the details even if it seems insignificant. This may act as a trigger to an overlooked memory. For example, "Please tell us everything that happened, from start to finish."
    - **Context reinstatement:** ask people to mentally place themselves at the scene of the event again and remember the environment exactly as it was, thereby triggering more detailed memories. For example, "Imagine you're back at the scene of the crime – what was the weather like?"
    - **Recall in reverse:** ask people to recall the events in a different order. This prevents them from saying what they expect to happen next in the list of events as it's harder to lie in reverse.
    - **Recall from a different perspective:** asked people to place themselves in a different person's perspective. This allows a more holistic view to be produced and prevents them from saying what they might expect to happen.
  - Fisher et al. reported results of 50 lab experiments that compared the cognitive interview and the standard interview. Participants were shown a film of a staged crime and were either given a cognitive or standard interview. Participants who received the cognitive interview recalled between 25–100% more correct information.

SNAPREVISE

Animal studies in attachment

- **Lorenz (1935): Imprinting in geese**
  - Lorenz collected gosling eggs and split them into two groups - he returned one group back to their mother and incubated the other group. When hatched, the first thing the incubated goslings saw was him, so viewed him as their 'mother' and followed him everywhere.
  - To test if they'd imprinted on him, he took the goslings back to the pond that they came from and reunited them with their biological mother. When Lorenz attempted to leave, the goslings followed him instead. They did not recognise nor attach to their biological mother.
  - From this study, he established a **critical period** of 2 days when animals imprint. If they do not imprint within these days, they will not at all.
  - He concluded that imprinting is innate and irreversible. It's used to bond with an adult caregiver in order for survival.
  - **Evaluation of Lorenz**
    - ◆ *Recent studies have shown imprinting could be reversible. It could be a learnt process rather than an innate mechanism.*
    - ◆ *Generalisability: many psychologists debate whether studies on birds can be generalised to humans due to the lack of similarity between species. Many argue this research is useless and does not account for the complexity of human emotions and relationships.*
- **Harlow (1959): Contact comfort in Rhesus monkeys**
  - Harlow created two artificial mothers for baby monkeys which he had orphaned. These mothers had different roles - one was cloth to provide comfort and the other was made of wire but had a feeding bottle. He recorded the amount of time that the baby's would spend on each.
  - He discovered that the baby monkeys spent the most time with the cloth mother as they sought out comfort when scared. These monkeys all developed abnormally due to a lack of biological mother and socialisation with other monkeys. As a result of this, they could never socialise normally with other monkeys. When approached by other monkeys, they reacted anxiously.
  - From his research, he developed a critical period of 3 months when attachment should be developed. If the attachment was formed later, there would be irreversible, harmful effects.
  - Harlow concluded that attachment wasn't based on food, but rather on a parent's ability to provide love and comfort.
  - **Evaluation of Harlow's research:**
    - ◆ *Ethical issues: Harlow has been criticised for animal cruelty. He orphaned newborn monkeys which lead them to grow abnormally. He would purposely scare them in order to test his hypothesis, causing psychological distress to the animals.*
    - ◆ *Confounding variable: this research has also been criticised for its lack of similarity in the shape of the fake mother's heads as the cloth mother looked more appealing. Therefore, the experiment has been criticised for not being standardised enough.*
    - ◆ *Generalisability: despite monkeys being genetically close to humans, people still question whether animal studies should be generalised to humans given our different levels of emotional complexity.*

Bowlby's theory of attachment

- **Bowlby (1969)** believed there must be an **innate and evolutionary** explanation for attachment which gives an **advantage for survival.**
- Key principles of Bowlby's theory:
  - Attachment is innate, adaptive, and monotropic.
    - **Innate:** attachment is a biological mechanism that gives us the drive to become attached from birth. Similarly, the mother is biologically programmed to love the child.
    - **Adaptive:** attachment has evolved to provide a baby with innate mechanisms from birth.
    - **Monotropic:** children cannot form multiple, meaningful attachments. Instead, they form one, special emotional bond to one specific person. The more time spent together, the stronger the bond will be. There are two main laws to this concept: the law of continuity and the law of accumulated separation:
      - **The law of continuity:** the more consistent and predictable care is for a child, the higher quality of the attachment.
      - **The law of accumulated separation:** the effects of every period of time where the mother is separated from her child will accumulate. Bowlby concluded that the ideal amount of separation is none.
  - **There are social releasers:** also known as 'baby behaviours' like crying or smiling that are intended to trigger caregiving.
  - **There is a critical period:** Harlow and others theorised this was approximately 2 years to form attachment.
  - **There is an internal working model:** this is a template for future relationships (i.e. loving caregiver leads to positive relationships).
- Evaluation of Bowlby's monotropic theory:
  - ◆ *Supported by **Brazelton et al. (1975)** who observed social releasers in the caregiver-baby 'interaction dance,' and by **Bailey et al. (2007)** who found that mothers with poor attachments often had infants with insecure attachments, supporting the internal working model.*
  - ◆ *Monotropy is debatable as evidence later showed that children can form multiple attachments, although the nature of attachment may vary.*

Learning theory

- **The learning theory:** states that behaviour is learnt and not innate: all behaviour is acquired through conditioning - operant or classical.
- **Classical conditioning:** when we unconsciously learn to associate a stimulus that brings a natural response to another, learnt stimulus to give the same response. This was demonstrated by **Ivan Pavlov (1897)** who outlined the process of classical conditioning in dogs:
  1. There is an **unconditioned stimulus** (food) that brings about an **unconditioned response** (dog drooling).
  2. The bell **(neutral stimulus)** is a new stimulus that doesn't lead to any response but is paired with the unconditioned stimulus to elicit the unconditioned response and make it a **conditioned response**.
  3. When the neutral stimulus has become associated with the unconditioned stimulus, it becomes a **conditioned stimulus**, which has a conditioned response (i.e. the dog expects food to appear when the bell rings, so the dog starts to drool at the bell even when there is no food).

- This theory has been applied to attachment where food is an unconditioned stimulus that elicits the unconditioned response of happiness in a baby, and the mother is a neutral stimulus that becomes conditioned over time so that the baby is happy upon seeing the mother, associating her presence with food.

- **Operant conditioning:** is a process that attempts to modify behaviour through the use of positive and negative reinforcement or punishment.
  - **Positive reinforcement:** when a desirable stimulus is added to encourage behaviour. In these situations, rewards are used to increase positive behaviour to ensure it continues (e.g. giving a child a sticker on a highly graded assessment).
  - **Negative reinforcement:** when an aversive stimulus is removed in order to encourage behaviour (e.g. a teacher ending detention early because the class was well-behaved).
  - **Positive punishment:** when an unfavourable consequence is added in order to weaken the response (e.g. giving a student a detention for misbehaving).
  - **Negative punishment:** removing something good after an undesired behaviour to try and stop the behaviour from being repeated (e.g. taking away a child's ice-cream for screaming).

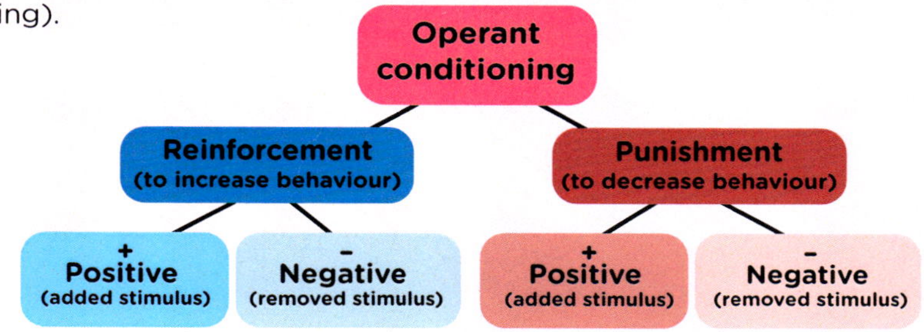

- Evaluation of the learning theory:
  - ◆ *Animal studies: the majority of learning theory is based on animal studies. This is a significant limitation of the research as humans are more complex and have higher levels of consciousness than animals, so this research may not be generalisable.*
  - ◆ *Simplistic: the assumption of reinforcement through feeding is too simplistic to fully explain attachment. Alternate research suggests that the responsiveness and attention offered by a parent may reinforce behaviour. Therefore, feeding alone cannot explain the bond between a parent and child. Additionally, the main feeder of a child may not always be the primary caregiver (e.g. a nanny may feed the child more often).*
  - ◆ ***Schaffer and Emerson (1964)** discovered that babies had formed a primary attachment to their mother even if they were not the main feeder. Their study showed that children formed the strongest attachment to the person who showed the most responsiveness to their emotional needs.*

Influence of early attachment

- Bowlby proposed that the **internal working model** acts as a cognitive schema for future relationships. A child who experiences a loving and reliable caregiver relationship forms a positive internal working model, expecting similar relationships in the future, while a child with an insecure attachment may expect rejection or untrustworthiness, leading to difficulties.
- Evidence supporting this continuity hypothesis includes the **Hazan and Shaver (1987)** 'Love Quiz' in which researches posted an ad in a US newspaper asking adults about their childhood attachment and current romantic experiences. They found that secure adults reported longer-lasting relationships, insecure-avoidant adults were more likely to fear intimacy, and insecure-resistant adults were more prone to jealousy. This suggests that early attachment influences adult romantic behaviour.
- Research also links childhood attachment to peer relationships: **Myron-Wilson and Smith (1998)** found that securely attached children were least likely to be involved in bullying, while insecure-resistant children were more likely to be bullies, and insecure-avoidant children more likely to be victims.
  - ◆ *Many studies are correlational, meaning that attachment type and later relationships are associated but causality cannot be established. Other factors like temperament or life experiences may play a more significant role.*
  - ◆ *Research relies on retrospective self-reports which may be inaccurate.*
  - ◆ *The theory has been criticised as overly deterministic, suggesting that early attachment fixes later outcomes, whereas evidence shows that insecurely attached individuals can still go on to form stable adult relationships.*

Ainsworth's Strange Situation

- **Ainsworth et al. (1978)** developed the Strange Situation, a structured observation designed to assess the quality of attachment between infants and their caregivers.
- The procedure involves seven episodes, including separations and reunions with the caregiver and the introduction of a stranger.
- Infant behaviours were assessed in terms of: **proximity seeking, exploration, stranger anxiety, separation anxiety,** and **reunion behaviour.**
- From this, Ainsworth identified three distinct types of attachment:
  - **Secure attachment** (about 60–75% of children) characterised by infants exploring freely but using the caregiver as a secure base, showing moderate separation and stranger anxiety, and being easily comforted upon reunion.
  - **Insecure-avoidant attachment** (around 20–25%) marked by a willingness to explore but little proximity-seeking, low separation, high stranger anxiety, and avoidance of the caregiver upon reunion.
  - **Insecure-resistant attachment** (about 3%) characterised by high levels of distress when separated, intense stranger anxiety, and ambivalent behaviour upon reunion, resisting comfort.
- The Strange Situation has been praised for its predictive validity. Attachment type has been linked to later outcomes, such as secure children developing better friendships and emotional health, while insecure attachments predict difficulties (**McCarthy, 1999**). It also demonstrates good inter-rater reliability, with **Bick et al. (2012)** reporting agreement among different observers of up to 94%.
- However, the procedure has been criticised as **culture-bound**. **Takahashi (1990)** found that Japanese infants were often classified as insecure-resistant because they showed extreme separation anxiety, but this reflected cultural norms where separation from mothers is rare, not genuine insecurity. In addition, the Strange Situation measures attachment to one caregiver, usually the mother, and may not reflect the infant's wider network of attachments.
- **Cultural variations:**
  - **Van Ijzendoorn and Kroonenberg (1988)** conducted a meta-analysis of 32 Strange Situation studies across eight countries. They found that secure attachment was the most common type in all cultures, supporting the claim that it is a universal norm. However, there were differences: in individualist cultures such as Germany, insecure-avoidant attachment was more common, while in collectivist cultures such as Japan, insecure-resistant attachment was more prevalent.
  - Interestingly, they also found that variation within cultures was 1.5 times greater than variation between cultures, suggesting that attachment styles differ significantly between subgroups (e.g. urban vs. rural; poor vs. wealthy) within the same culture.

Bowlby's theory of maternal deprivation

- **Bowlby's (1951)** theory of **maternal deprivation** proposed that continuous, quality attachment with a caregiver during the first two and a half years (the **critical period**) is essential for healthy psychological development.
- Deprivation refers to the loss of attachment due to prolonged separation, which Bowlby argued could lead to **intellectual delay** and **emotional problems.** A key emotional consequence is **affectionless psychopathy**, where individuals show little guilt or empathy, making it difficult to form normal relationships.
- Bowlby's **44 Thieves Study** compared 44 young people convicted of stealing with 44 young people who were also in a delinquency centre but with no record of stealing. They found that 17 thieves had experienced prolonged separation from their mothers during early childhood. Of these 17, there were 15 juvenile thieves who were classified as affectionless psychopaths. This supports the view that deprivation can have serious long-term effects.
  - ◆ *The study has been criticised for* **methodological flaws**. *Bowlby carried out the assessments himself, creating a risk of researcher bias, and the study was correlational, so we cannot be certain deprivation caused the outcomes.*
  - ◆ *Later research, such as* ***Rutter (1981),*** *distinguished between* **privation** *(failure to form an attachment at all) and* **deprivation,** *arguing that some of the severe consequences Bowlby described were more likely due to privation. Despite criticisms, Bowlby's theory had significant real-world impact, changing hospital practices by ensuring children were not separated from parents for long periods.*

Effects of institutionalisation

- Research into institutionalisation investigates the impact of children being raised in orphanages or institutions with minimal emotional care.
- The most influential work is **Rutter et al.'s (2011)** English and Romanian Adoptees project. Rutter followed 165 Romanian orphans adopted by British families, assessing their development at ages 4, 6, 11, and 15. Children adopted before the age of 6 months showed normal development, while those adopted after 6 months displayed disinhibited attachment, characterised by attention-seeking and indiscriminate affection, as well as cognitive delays. By age 11, some recovery had occurred, particularly for those adopted earlier, suggesting the existence of a **sensitive period** rather than an absolute critical period for forming attachments.
  - ◆ *A strength of Rutter's study is its* ***longitudinal design****, allowing researchers to track development over time. It has also had practical applications, improving childcare systems and emphasising the importance of consistent caregiving. However, the Romanian orphanages involved were unusually deprived (e.g. low resources, poor nutrition), so findings may not generalise to all institutions. Moreover, not all institutionalised children experienced negative outcomes, highlighting the role of individual differences and resilience.*
  - ◆ *Other research, such as* ***Zeanah et al. (2005)*** *using the Strange Situation on institutionalised children, found high rates of disinhibited attachment compared to controls. These findings demonstrate that institutionalisation can lead to long-term emotional and cognitive difficulties if adoption or fostering is delayed.*

SNAPREVISE

Overview of the approaches

Approach	Methods of investigation	Issues and debates
Biological	Highly scientific lab studies	Nature, determinism, scientific
Cognitive	Experimental/lab studies	Nature, soft determinism, scientific
Behaviourism	Experimental/lab studies, animal studies	Nurture, determinism, scientific
Social learning theory	Observation	Nurture, less deterministic, scientific
Humanistic	Abstract concepts found discussion	Nurture, not deterministic, not scientific
Psychodynamic	Intensive case studies and dream analysis	Nature, deterministic, not scientific

The biological approach

- **Key concepts:**
  - Everything psychological is first biological. In order to understand human behaviour, we need to look at biological structures.
  - Links to evolutionary theories to explain how humans have evolved and adapted in order to survive or reproduce.
- **Genotypes vs. phenotypes:** a genotype is our genetic makeup. A phenotype is the way our genes are expressed.
- **The evolutionary perspective on behaviour:**
  - The biological approach looks at how natural and sexual selection has led to adaptations of physical and psychological characteristics on behaviour today.
  - Psychologists will try to understand why these characteristics come about and the effect that they have on people today (e.g. women attempting to look younger to appear more fertile and thus attractive to men to fulfil a biological desire for reproduction).
- **The brain and neurochemistry:**
  - Psychologists explore the structure of the brain and how neurochemistry effects behaviour. This includes the effects of neurotransmitters such as serotonin and dopamine and how hormones can affect our behaviour (e.g. testosterone causing aggression).
  - Cognitive neuroscience is the scientific study of the influence of brain structure on mental processes. Brain mapping is used to identify specific cognitive functions in different brain areas. This has been done recently through the use of PET and fMRI scans. This research has also led psychologists to establish the neurological basis of many mental disorders.
    - ◆ *Reliable: provides reliable and clear predictions about the effects of neurotransmitters and hormones in the brain. This has led to greater research on psychoactive drugs and their effects, and in turn lead to greater treatments that help neurochemical abnormalities.*
    - ◆ *Scientific: uses highly scientific methods to carry out research such as MRI scanning, brain imaging, and genetic screening. They can be easily replicated, meaning they have high objectivity and validity.*
    - ◆ *Too deterministic: this approach claims all behaviour is the result of genes and other internal biological causes which we have no control over. This means that we may have no control over our actions, and has dangerous implications for criminality.*

The cognitive approach

- The cognitive approach is a response to the behaviourists' lack of explanation for people's mental processes.
- **Key concepts:**
  - It focuses on how people perceive, store, interpret, and use information and how it affects behaviour, mainly based on information processing – information is taken in by the senses and then processed in the brain, then stored and retrieved when needed.
  - It proposed that humans use mental tools like schemas to make judgements.
  - It only uses experimental studies for research so it is considered to be scientific.
  - It often uses computer metaphors to explain mental processes and has been greatly enabled by technological advances.
- **Schemas:** mental frameworks of beliefs and expectations that are used to help interpret information about the world efficiently.
  - They are developed from our experiences and what we have seen in the past.
  - They can help 'fill in gaps' when we lack information about something and if we receive information that contradicts our schemas, we often disregard it.
  - Advancements in computer programming have led to psychologists to focusing more on the way information is stored and retrieved.
    - ◆ *Scientific credibility: they use highly controlled methods of study such as lab experiments to allow researched to make inferences about cognition. They use specific lab equipment such as brain scanners which produce reliable and strictly objective data.*
    - ◆ *Soft determinism: regarded as less strict than hard determinism. The cognitive approach recognised that our cognitive system can only function within its biological limits that are out of our control; however, we are free to react and think about stimuli.*
    - ◆ *Real world application: cognitive therapy is the main choice of therapy that the NHS provides to people in need of help with depression, OCD, and anxiety*
    - ◆ *Machine reductionism: the cognitive approach treats the human mind like a computer and ignores the influence of human emotion on the cognitive system.*

The learning approach – behaviourism

- **Key principles:**
  - All behaviour is learnt, not innate.
  - Psychology should only be studied in a scientific manner.
  - Focus should be on controlling observable and measurable behaviour, not internal things like thinking and emotions.
  - Animal studies can and should be generalised to humans as learning is the same across species.
  - Leaning takes place through classical and operant conditioning.
- **Skinner (1948):** conducted experiments with rats and pigeons in specially designed cages called Skinner boxes. Every time a rat activated a lever (or pecked a disc in the case of the pigeon) within the box, a food pellet was released. This would result in the animal performing the behaviour again and again to gain the food pellet, therefore reinforcing that particular behaviour from the animal. He also conditioned the animals behaviour to avoid an unpleasant stimulus (using an electric shock).
  - ◆ *Scientific credibility: by emphasising the importance of the need for objectivity and reproducibility, behaviourism played a key role in the development of psychology as a scientific discipline.*
  - ◆ *Real world application: the principles of operant conditioning have been applied to real world situations (e.g. schools using a sticker reward system to incentivise good student behaviour).*
  - ◆ *Deterministic: Skinner claimed that humans have no control over their own behaviour, and argued that all behaviour was as a result of past experiences and conditioning. He argued that free will is an illusion, which many view as excessively deterministic.*
  - ◆ *Ethical issues: some argue that Skinner's experiments constituted animal cruelty by causing both physical and psychological harm to animals in breach of psychological guidelines.*

The learning approach – social learning theory

- **Albert Bandura (1977)** proposed the social learning theory as a development of the behaviourist approach. He generally agreed with the key principles of the behaviourist approach (that all behaviour is learned through experience) but he argued that conditioning could not explain all human learning. He claimed that there were important cognitive or mental processes that mediate between the stimulus and response and added that whilst people do learn directly through conditioning they also learn indirectly by observing and imitating others.
- **Vicarious reinforcement:** people learn indirectly through vicarious reinforcement. This is when people can learn behaviour through observation and imitation of others as they see the consequences of this behaviour.
- **The meditational processes:**
  - Attention: you have to pay attention to the model's behaviour to learn it through observing
  - Retention: you have to remember the behaviour
  - Reproduction: you need to be physically able to reproduce the modelled behaviour
  - Motivation: this is the final step where an individual decides to replicate the behaviour they have observed in order to get a reward or punishment.
- We usually choose to replicate behaviour from someone we look up to, such as a role model. Role models are someone we identify with, relate to, and want to be like. Identification is when we relate to someone, and recognise a similarity or something better in them, so we learn from their behaviour and emulate it.
- **Bandura's (1961)** Bobo doll experiment:
  - Bandura recorded the behaviour of young children who had watched an adult behave in an aggressive manner towards a Bobo doll. The adults were filmed punching, hitting, kicking the Bobo doll. Then, the child had to watch the video of the adult hurting the doll. Later, Bandura placed the children individually into a room with a Bobo doll. Those who had seen the punching video acted more aggressively towards the doll than those who hadn't seen the video.
  - He repeated his experiment with three conditions: in one condition, the adult was seen being rewarded for their aggressive behaviour, in another the adult was seen being punished for their behaviour, and in the final condition the adult was seen being aggressive with no consequence. He discovered that the children in the first condition acted the most aggressively towards the doll afterwards, then the third group, and finally the second group acted the least aggressively.
    - ◆ *Less deterministic than the learning approach: the learning approach argues that all behaviour is learnt through a type of conditioning that is forced onto us. However, Bandura argues the case of reciprocal determinism where we are influenced by our environment, but we also have an impact on others in our environment too. He also argues that although we are heavily influenced by our environment as a child, when we grow older we are able to choose how to behave more freely.*
    - ◆ *Low external validity: doesn't mention any biological factors that could have affected his experiment. For instance, in the experiment, boys were seen to be significantly more aggressive than girls. This can be explained by differences in hormone levels as boys have a naturally higher level of testosterone than girls, which has been associated with aggressive behaviour. Bandura doesn't mention this factor at all which makes it a possible extraneous variable.*
    - ◆ *Demand characteristics: despite his research being highly controlled, this research has been criticised for promoting his participants to respond in the way he wanted to, meaning the children may have only responded in this way as they wanted to please Bandura or do what the experiment expected of them.*

Approaches in psychology

SNAPREVISE

The psychodynamic approach

- **Freud (1923):** focused on the role of the unconscious mind and its effect on our behaviour.
- **The structure of personality:** Freud claimed that our personality is made up of 3 parts that all have different motives and desires. They all conflict and fight for priority.
  - **Id:** operates on the unconscious. It controls libido and functions based on the pleasure principle. It demands immediate gratification and is thus responsible for our impulsivity.
  - **Ego:** operates on the reality principle. It mediates between impulsive demands of the id and the requirements of the superego and the external world.
  - **Superego:** develops our sense of morality and judgement between wrong and right. It gives us our ability to feel guilt for our actions, operating on the morality principle.
- **Coping mechanisms:** Freud claimed that when we are faced with a situation we can't deal with or resolve, we use unconscious defence mechanisms which distort reality to reduce anxiety and negative emotions. They are considered unhealthy in the long run. They are:
  - **Repression:** we take the memory causing us stress and force it out of our conscious mind.
  - **Denial:** we refuse to acknowledge that this event occurred.
  - **Displacement:** we take out our negative emotions on a different target.
- **The psycho-sexual stages of development:**
  - **Oral stage (0–1 year):** the mouth is the focus point of pleasure and the mothers breast is the hyperfixation – the consequence of unresolved conflict during this time would be developing an oral fixation later in life such as smoking or biting nails.
  - **Anal stage (1–3 years):** focus point of pleasure is the anus – this is linked to toilet training as the child begins to learn how to use the bathroom by themselves. During this time the ego is starting to develop and the child becomes aware of the demands of others. The consequence of unresolved conflict during this time would be the person becoming anal retentive (excessively organised) or anal expulsive (excessively messy) later in life.
  - **Phallic stage (3–5 years):** the focus point of pleasure is the genitals – linked to the 'Oedipus complex' where the son unconsciously wishes to possess his mother and replace his father. The consequence of unresolved conflict during this time is developing a narcissistic personality later in life.
  - **Latent stage (5 years to puberty):** conflicts become repressed.
  - **Genital stage (puberty to adulthood):** sexual desires become apparent during puberty. The consequence of unresolved conflict during this time would be difficultly developing heterosexual relationships.
    - ◆ *Freud was one of the first psychologists to explore the importance of childhood, drawing links between childhood behaviour and how that has an impact on behaviour later in life. His work is arguably the foundation for the modern understanding of the unconscious mind.*
    - ◆ *Based on case studies: his work lacks generalisability as his theories were heavily based on a few individuals. His observations were very detailed and thorough, but modern psychologists have argued that we cannot make universal claims based on information from a few people. Additionally, the people he studied were particularly abnormal so likely not representative of the general population.*
    - ◆ *Lacks scientific credibility: his theories are broadly based on the unconscious mind which we cannot directly view or study due to the ambiguous nature of it. The claims are not falsifiable and cannot be empirically tested so are not scientific.*
    - ◆ *Freud's theories overemphasise the importance of sex and approach psychological development from a Western and heteronormative lens that may not be not generalisable to the broader population.*

The humanistic approach

- Developed by **Maslow and Rogers (1943),** the humanistic approach emphasises the importance of personal growth and fulfilment, focusing on personal responsibility.
- It is less scientific but observes the individual as a whole, including their emotions, feelings, motivations, etc.
- Key principles include self-actualisation and the hierarchy of needs:

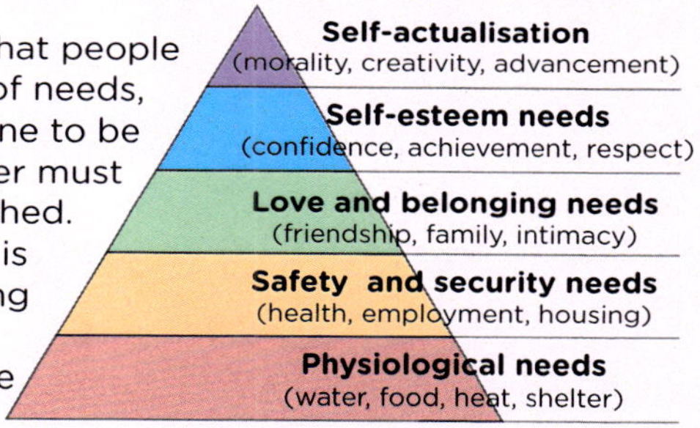

  - Maslow claimed that people have a hierarchy of needs, and in order for one to be addressed, another must first be accomplished.
  - Self-actualisation is the most rewarding human need. When people have self-actualised, they have no anxiety; they are creative, constantly happy, and feel at peace with themselves.
  - Rogers argued that for personal growth to be accomplished, an individual must seek congruence. This is when their self and ideal self are aligned which gives them a feeling of self-worth.
  - He believed that our feelings around self-worth and self-acceptance are based on our interactions with others, specifically our parents.
  - If these people have high expectations of us (conditions of worth) that we cannot to live up to in order to gain positive regard or achieve acceptance, then we develop incongruence which stops us from reaching self-actualisation.
- Free will: promotes the idea that we all have autonomy and can choose our own life/destiny.
    - ◆ *Abstract ideas: the humanistic approach is based on largely abstract and unfalsifiable ideas. The subjective ideas of 'congruence' and 'self-actualisation' cannot be proven and therefore lack scientific credibility.*
    - ◆ *Little real world application: despite counselling techniques being developed from this idea, there is minimal other applications for us in real-world situations.*

The nervous system

The nervous system is separated into two divisions: the central nervous system and the peripheral nervous system.

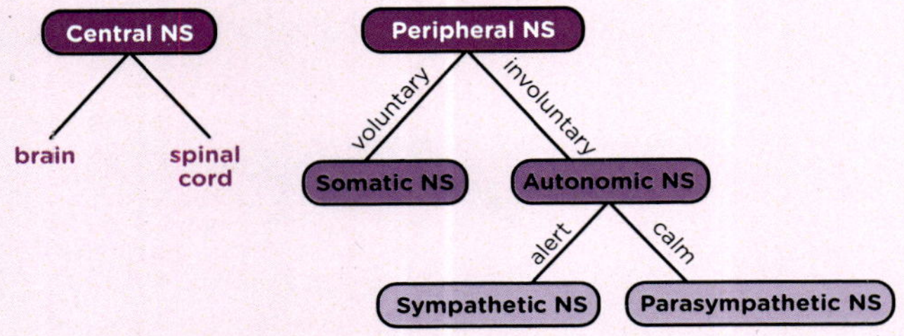

- **The central nervous system:**
  - **The brain:** receives and process information from the senses. It contains our conscious awareness, imitates responses, stores memories, and generates emotions and thoughts.
  - **The spinal cord:** conducts signals to and from the brain. It controls our reflex actions.
- **The peripheral nervous system:** sends messages to and from the central nervous system via neurons and is separated into two parts: the autonomic nervous system and the somatic nervous system.
  - **The autonomic nervous system:** involuntary responses. This system only has motor pathways and doesn't directly control effectors. It's separated into the sympathetic branch and the parasympathetic branch:
    - **Sympathetic branch:** the fight or flight response that prepares the body to confront a threat when stressed.
    - **Sympathetic branch:** restores and conserves the body's energy when relaxed or after a threat has passed.
  - **The somatic nervous system:** voluntary movements. This system is made up of motor and sensory pathways, and it can control effectors directly.

Structure and functions of neurons

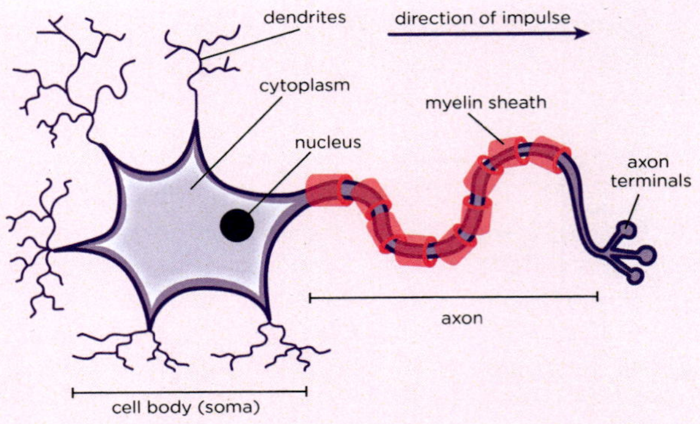

- There are billions of nerve cells called neurons that make up the nervous system. They communicate with one another by using electrical and chemical signals.
- **The structure of a neuron:**
  - Cell membrane: the wall of the cell.
  - Dendrites: carry nerve impulses from neighbouring neurons towards the cell body.
  - Cell body: contains the genetic material of the cell.
  - Axon: plays a major role in communication between neurons. It carries impulses away from the cell body down the neuron. It's covered in a fatty layer called the myelin sheath that speeds up electrical transmission and protects the axon.
  - Terminal buttons: communicates with the next neurone in the chain across a synapse.
- Three types of neuron:
  - **Sensory neuron:** sends information from the senses (ANS) through to the brain (CNS). Receptors are found in eyes, mouth, ears, and skin. They have long dendrites and short axons.
  - **Relay neuron:** connect sensory neurons to motor neurons or other relay neurons via the CNS. They analyse sensations from the neurons and decide how to respond. They have short dendrites and short axons.
  - **Motor neurons:** send information via the axons from the brain through to effectors (e.g. muscles or glands). They have long axons and short dendrites.
- **Synaptic transmission:**
  - The process of synaptic transmission begins in the pre-synaptic neuron. Action potentials are sent down the axon until they reach the pre-synaptic terminal. Information can only travel in one direction at a synapse. This is because chemical messengers can only bind to specific reception sites.
  - Neurotransmitters are stored in vesicles. The action potentials cause the release of neurotransmitters to be released into the pre-synaptic cleft.
  - These neurotransmitters then diffuse across the synaptic gap and bind with specific receptor sites that are only available on the post-synaptic neuron.
  - Once there's enough neurotransmitters on the post-synaptic neuron, two things may occur: the next neuron may be ready to fire, depending on whether the neurotransmitter had an exhibitor or inhibitory effect in the neuron, or re-uptake may occur. This is where neurotransmitters are stored in vesicles on the pre-synaptic neuron.
  - Excitatory neurotransmitters (e.g. adrenaline) are chemical messengers that makes it more likely that the next neuron will fire an impulse down its axon.
  - Inhibitory neurotransmitters (e.g. serotonin) reduce the likelihood that neurons will fire an impulse down an axon.
  - Summation occurs when the excitatory and inhibitory effects are added together.

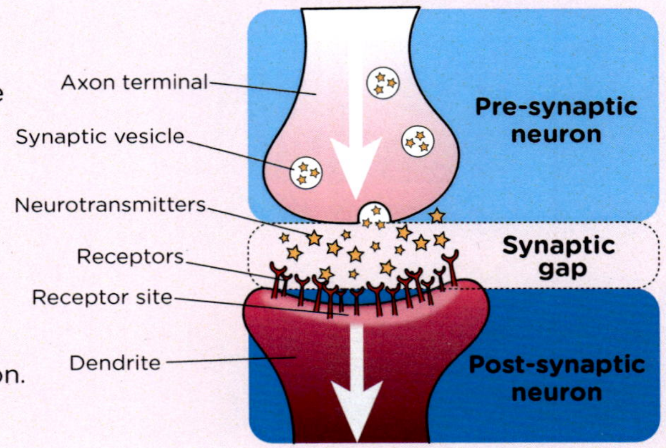

The endocrine system

- **The endocrine system:** is made up of glands and hormones which all have specific roles in the body. These hormones regulate bodily functions and create a chemical communication system via the bloodstream. It's slower than the nervous system, but its effects are more widespread.
- **Glands:** an organ that releases specific hormones for use in the body. Hormones are chemical messengers that are released by glands into the bloodstream. The glands you need to know are:
  - **Pituitary gland:** the 'master gland' that secrets a multitude of hormones that all have different functions in the body. These hormones control the functions of other glands. For example, the pituitary gland release the hormones FSH and LH which allow for the release of testosterone from the testes to the body. These hormones encourage the development of sperm and male sex characteristics. The anterior pituitary gland releases FSH and LH which encourage the ovaries to release progesterone and oestrogen to regulate the menstrual cycle and prepare the female body for reproduction.
  - **The adrenal gland:** releases adrenaline which triggers the fight or flight response which causes physiological changes to our bodies (e.g. wider pupils, an inactive gut, and increased blood flow to the brain).

Fight or flight response

- The fight or flight response is a biological human response to a detected stressor. Humans are built to have an immediate reaction when faced with danger: to stay and fight the threat or to run away.
- Both the autonomic nervous system and the endocrine system play major roles in this response. The sympathetic branch is activated when a stressor is identified.
- The process of fight or flight response is:
  1. A stressor is identified but the hypothalamus and activates the parasympathetic branch of the ANS.
  2. The adrenal medulla releases adrenaline and noradrenaline into the bloodstream.
  3. The release of adrenaline leads to physiological changes in the body, such as increased heart rate, increased respiration and it diverts blood away from the skins surface and towards more vital organs.
  4. This is the fight or flight response which prepares the body for sudden reaction.
  5. Once the stressor has been removed, the parasympathetic branch returns the body back to normal.

  ◆ *Modern research suggests there may be more than just these two responses of fight or flight (e.g. the 'fight, flight, freeze, fawn, flop' model accounts for 'freezing' where a person cannot move against a threat, 'fawning' where a person seeks to please someone to avoid conflict, and 'flopping' where a person faints or becomes unresponsive when confronted by a threat).*

Ways of studying the brain

- **Functional magnetic imaging resonance (FMRI):** works by identifying changes in levels of oxygen in the blood that occur as a result of brain activity in specific areas. When an area is more active than another, there will be increased blood flow to that area. It produces a 3D image called an **activation map** that shows which part is active. This has been used to identify which areas play a role in specific mental processes.
  - ◆ *fMRIs are safer than most brain scans and are non-invasive. They also do not use radiation, which can harm our body cells.*
  - ◆ *It has a high spatial resolution so can clearly see the specific location where brain activity takes place. However, it has low temporal resolution because there is a time delay from the scanner to the image, lowering internal validity.*
- **Electroencephalogram (EEG):** involves a cap of electrodes being placed on the skull that detects small electrical changes resulting from the activity of brain cells. These charges are graphed over time to see a person's average brain activity. They're mainly used to detect **sleep patterns** and used as a **diagnostic tool** to help diagnose conditions like epilepsy.
  - ◆ *High temporal resolution: you see signals within a millisecond so you receive results quickly.*
  - ◆ *Low spatial resolution: you cannot pinpoint where the brain activity is taking place which makes the results overall less valuable.*
- **Event-related potentials (ERP):** electrodes are placed on the scalp to measure brain activity. ERPs show **specific brain activity** as all extraneous brain activity is filtered out from the original recording. It leaves only the brain's responses to the active stimulus that they were presented with. They are usually used to measure **attention and perception.**
  - ◆ *High temporal resolution: there is no time delay and is specific to the time that it's happening.*
  - ◆ *Low spatial resolution: cannot pinpoint where the brain activity is taking place.*
  - ◆ *Extraneous noise: cannot always obtain meaningful data due to extraneous variables such as background noise, so may lack internal validity.*
- **Post-mortems:** the brain of a dead patient is removed and dissected to look for any physical abnormalities. This can be compared to a healthy brain that doesn't have a particular condition. This is usually used for people with **rare conditions or defects.**
  - ◆ *Allow for an in-depth analysis of the brain: researchers may get to explore and develop theories that previously they couldn't due to the fact some brain areas would be too deep to see otherwise, such as the hypothalamus.*
  - ◆ *There's no cause and effect: damage to the brain cannot be linked to a specific cause as the patient is dead, so the research is subject to extraneous variables, and obviously cannot be used to treat the patient themselves.*

SNAPREVISE

Localisation of function in the brain

- **Localisation of function:** specific areas of the brains are specialised for certain functions.
- **Broca's area (left hemisphere):** is responsible for production of spoken and written language. If this area gets damaged, it can result in **Broca's aphasia** where a person may have slowed speech that lacks fluency, or a total absence of speech.
- **Wernicke's area (left hemisphere):** this area is responsible for the understanding of language. Damage to this area can cause **Wernicke's aphasia** where people cannot understand spoken language or can only produce nonsense words/phrases.
- **Motor cortex (both hemispheres):** is responsible for voluntary motor movements. Damage to this area can cause a loss of control of fine movements on the opposite side of the body.
- **Visual cortex (both hemispheres):** this area receives information from the eyes. Damage to this area can cause hallucinations or blindness.
- **Auditory cortex (both hemispheres):** this area is responsible for analysing speech based on information. Damage to this area can result in partial or complete hearing loss.
- **Somatosensory cortex (both hemispheres):** this area is responsible for processing information from the senses. Damage to this area can cause problems in processing touch.
    - ***Paul Broca's (1861)*** *study of a patent known as 'Tan' led to the discovery of Broca's area. The patient could understand spoken language but couldn't produce any coherent words – he could only say 'Tan.' A post-mortem was conducted after Tan's death, and Broca discovered a lesion on his left frontal lobe. This case study supports localisation of function as it shows that when damage is caused to specific areas of the brain, their functions can no longer be carried out properly.*
    - ***Carl Wernicke (1874)*** *discovered that patients with lesions to the Wernicke's area, located in the left temporal lobe, were still able to speak but couldn't comprehend language. People with damage to this area struggled to comprehend language – they often produced sentences that were fluent but lacked meaning.*

Hemispheric lateralisation and split brain research

- **Split brain theory:** the brain is split into two halves called the left and right hemisphere. It's believed that different areas of the brains are responsible for different mental processes.
- **The left hemisphere:** receives information from and controls the right side of the body. It receives information from the right visual field. Language is lateralised to the left for the majority of people.
- **The right hemisphere:** receives information from and controls the left side of the body. It receives information from the left visual field. It provides the emotional context of speech.
- Many functions are not lateralised to specific hemispheres; for example, vision and motor areas can be found in both hemispheres. The two hemispheres are joined together by a corpus callosum which allows them to communicate which each other. Patients with severe epilepsy may have their corpus collosum severed. Their hemispheres then became functionally separate.
    - ***Sperry and Gazzaniga's (1967)*** *split brain research examined 11 patients who had all had their corpus callosum severed. He presented information to either their left or right visual field for 1/10th of a second, noting that when information was presented to the left visual field, subjects could draw it but not name it, whereas in the right visual field, they could name the object both in writing and verbally. This supports hemispheric lateralisation as it demonstrates that the hemispheres have different functions.*
    - ***Danelli et al. (2013)*** *examined a patient called EB – a young boy who had almost all of the left hemisphere of his brain removed at age two and lost complete language abilities. However, this case study also challenges split brain theory as he regained some language ability with other brain areas taking over the function.*

Plasticity and functional recovery after trauma

- **Plasticity:** the brain's ability to change and adapt its structure based on experience and new learning.
- **Synaptic pruning:** during infancy, over 15,000 synaptic connections are created, which is twice as many as the adult brain. Synaptic connections that are not used regularly as we age are deleted and ones that are used regularly are strengthened. For instance, **Maguire et al. (2000)** studied London cab drivers who complete a test called 'the knowledge' which assesses their recall of city streets and routes. She found that people who had been taxi drivers for longer had more grey matter in their posterior hippocampus than those who had only done it for a short time.
- **Functional recovery:** a type of plasticity that refers to recovery of abilities and mental processes that have been affected as a result of brain damage or disease. The brain can rewire itself by forming new synaptic connections close to the damaged area. Then, secondary neural pathways will be activated to enable functioning to continue. This creates structural differences in the brain. This may occur very quickly after trauma, and then slow down over time.
    - **Axonal sprouting:** the growth of new nerve endings to form new neural pathways.
    - **Recruitment of homologous areas:** opposite side of the brain takes over the function of damaged area.
- **Factors affecting recovery after trauma:**
    - Gender: females may be more likely to have better recovery than males.
    - Age: younger people are more likely to recover from damage than older people. This may be linked to the deterioration of the brain in older age.
    - Perseverance: people who try harder to recover are more likely to recover. Many people give up on recovery as they believe it isn't possible.
    - Stress and alcohol: a higher intake of alcohol can make it harder for someone to recover due to a lack of effort put towards recovery. Stress can also delay recovery due to the energy that is consumed with anxiety rather than recovery.

Definitions in the field of mental health

- **Statistical infrequency:** a disorder is abnormal if it is more than 2 standard deviations away from a mean incidence rate on a normally-distributed bell curve model.
- **The failure to function adequately:** **Rosenhan and Seligman (1989)** suggested that if a person's mental state stops them from living a normal life and carrying out everyday tasks, then they may be considered as abnormal. They don't follow typical social rules, they may be in distress, and their behaviour can be considered reckless.
- **Deviation from norms:** 'abnormal' behaviour is when people stray away from social or cultural norms. These are based on general social and cultural norms.
- **Deviation from ideal mental health:** proposed by **Jahoda (1958)** who looked at what would comprise someone's normal mental health. He based it on criteria that would lead people to be unable to self-actualise or have an inaccurate perception of themselves. These people wouldn't be able to carry out everyday tasks and display low self-esteem.
- **Characteristics of phobias:**
  - **Behavioural characteristics:**
    - **Panic:** a heightened physiological arousal when presented with a specific stressor/phobic stimulus. This is caused by the hypothalamus triggering the sympathetic branch of the autonomic nervous system.
    - **Avoidance:** negatively reinforces the phobia as the person actively avoids the stimulus to avoid the unpleasant consequence. This therefore affects the individual's ability to live their life normally.
    - **Endurance:** the patient is exposed to the phobic stimulus for a long duration of time. They will experience intense anxiety.
  - **Emotional characteristics:** anxiety and being unaware that the anxiety you get when exposed to it is irrational.
  - **Cognitive characteristics:** selective attention (remains focused on the stimuli even when experiencing intense anxiety), irrational beliefs (incorrect perception of what the danger is), and cognitive distortions (doesn't perceive the stimulus accurately, so it will appear distorted).
- **Characteristics of depression:**
  - **Behavioural characteristics:** decreased energy levels, aggression (often irrational), and changed patterns of eating and sleeping.
  - **Emotional characteristics:** low self-esteem, consistent poor mood, and intense, uncontrollable anger.
  - **Cognitive characteristics:** black-and-white thinking, paying the most attention to negative events, and poor concentration.
- **Characteristics of obsessive compulsive disorder (OCD):**
  - **Behavioural characteristics:** compulsions and avoidance behaviour.
  - **Emotional characteristics:** guilt, depression, anxiety, and disgust.
  - **Cognitive characteristics:** obsessive thoughts and acknowledging that their anxiety is irrational.

Behavioural approach

- **The behavioural approach to explaining phobias:**
  - Phobias are created through classical conditioning and maintained through operant conditioning.
  - Avoidance behaviour is negatively reinforced - when they avoid the fear-evoking stimulus they are reinforcing their fear through a lack of exposure.
  - **Watson and Rayner's (1920)** Little Albert experiment created association in a small child by showing him a white rat (neutral stimulus) and making a loud bang (unconditioned stimulus), which caused fear (unconditioned response), and repeating it several times. The subject then created an association between the rat (now conditioned stimulus), and the loud bang by showing fear (now conditioned response).
    - ◆ *Face validity: the Little Albert explanation works at face value to explain why people create and retain phobias. It makes sense to us that avoiding a phobic stimulus would reinforce the phobia rather than solve it.*
    - ◆ *Ethical implications: this experiment caused long lasting psychological harm to a young child which violates ethical standards.*
- **The behavioural approach to treating phobias:**
  - **Systematic desensitisation:** aims to treat phobias through gradual expose to the phobic stimulus. It uses the idea of counterconditioning to rewire the patient's brain. The patient and therapist create an anxiety hierarchy which ranks events that would cause anxiety involving the phobic stimulus. Then, the patient is taught relaxation techniques to help ease their anxiety when exposed to the stimulus. The phobia is believed to be cured when a person can reach the highest level (e.g. leaving the house for an agoraphobic person), and can effectively calm themselves down.
    - ◆ *Systematic desensitisation is more suitable for those with learning disabilities: flooding may be too overwhelming for neurodiverse people or people with disabilities, whereas working through a phobia step-by-step can be more logical and effective.*
    - ◆ *Lowered attrition rates: since it is seen as more effective, people are more likely to succeed with this therapy and not require ongoing treatment.*
  - **Flooding:** an alternate technique to systematic desensitisation that immerses the patient in their phobia and 'floods' their senses with it (e.g. placing someone with arachnophobia in a room full of spiders for a prolonged period of time). This creates high levels of anxiety, but after the anxiety reaches its peak, it will decrease. By doing this, the patient learns that the phobic stimulus is harmless.
    - ◆ *Cost effective and quick: it takes a shorter amount of planning and time to complete than systematic desensitisation.*
    - ◆ *May not work for complex phobias: cognitive therapy may be more effective for those with social phobias as they are believed to be more complex.*

SNAPREVISE

Cognitive approach

- **The cognitive approach to explaining depression:**
  - **Beck (1967)** theorised that some people have a cognitive vulnerability to developing depression through faulty information processing, negative self-schemas, and the cognitive triad of automatic negative thought. Faulty information processing leads to a patient catastrophising small problems and thinking in black and white terms. Negative self-schemas lead them to believe everything about them is negative which lowers self-esteem. This leads them to believe negative thoughts about themselves, the future, and the world.
    - ◆ *This lead to more cognitive therapies being developed and the strategy of therapists challenging irrational thoughts. It therefore helps to prove the efficacy of CBT.*
  - **Ellis' (1957)** ABC model consists of:
    - (A) an activating effect that offsets the development of depression.
    - (B) an irrational belief that brings about the effect of depression.
    - (C) an emotional consequence of depression.
    - ◆ *Practical application: CBT therapy aims to challenge irrational beliefs which is supported by Ellis' theory.*
    - ◆ *Not all depression starts with an activation event – some types of depression are reactive or don't have a noticeable cause.*
- The cognitive approach to treating depression:
  - Cognitive behavioural therapy (CBT) aims to identify and then challenge irrational thoughts by replacing them with helpful behaviours.
  - **Beck's (1994)** CBT focused on identifying irrational beliefs and challenging them. The cognitive triad comes in useful here to help guide the therapy as the patient can name exactly what they're worried about.
  - Tests reality of their beliefs: patients are often instructed to keep a diary of their week and record every positive interaction they had with someone. Therefore, when a patient says that everyone hates them or has a negative outlook on the world, the therapist can challenge their thoughts and beliefs.
  - **Ellis' (1955)** rational emotive behaviour therapy: aims to identify the patient's thoughts and challenge them as irrational. It tries to break a link between negative life events and depression.

Biological approach

- **The biological approach to explaining OCD:**
  - **Genetic explanations:**
    - **Candidate genes:** certain genes are linked with vulnerability to OCD (e.g. the SERT gene affecting serotonin transport, COMT gene affecting dopamine regulation, 5HT1-D beta which affects the efficiency of serotonin transport across the synapse).
    - **Polygenic:** OCD is not caused by a single gene but multiple genes. Each gene only increases risk slightly. **Taylor (2013)** discovered that OCD is polygenic which means that 230 different genes are involved in its development.
    - **Aetiologically heterogeneous:** different gene combinations may lead to different types of OCD (e.g. hoarding vs. contamination).
    - **Family and twin studies: the** higher concordance rates for OCD in identical (MZ) twins than non-identical (DZ) twins suggests genetic influence, though this rate is not 100%. **Lewis (1936)** found that of his OCD patients, 37% had parents with OCD and 21% had siblings with OCD.
  - **Neural explanations:**
    - **Neurotransmitters:** low serotonin activity leads to impaired mood regulation, which is linked to OCD. High dopamine activity is also associated with compulsive behaviours.
    - **Brain circuits:** overactivity in the basal ganglia and orbitofrontal cortex is linked to repetitive thoughts and compulsions. Thalamus hyperactivity may reinforce compulsive checking behaviours.
- **The biological approach to treating OCD:**
  - The main drug treatments used are selective serotonin reuptake inhibitors (SSRIs) which prevent the reuptake and breakdown of serotonin on the pre-synaptic neuron. This leads to an increase in the concentration of serotonin in the synapse and therefore the post-synaptic neuron is constantly stimulated.
  - Tricyclics have a similar effect but are mainly used for people who don't find SSRIs effective or have bad reactions to them. They increase the concentration of noradrenaline neurotransmitter in the brain.
    - ◆ *Drug therapy can cause very bad side effects: patients taking clomipramine can suffer from side effects such as tremors, fatigue, aggressiveness, and weight gain.*
    - ◆ *Drug therapy and the economy: when people start being treated by drugs, they are less likely to miss days of work as they have more of a grasp on their condition compared to if they are unmedicated.*

SNAPREVISE

Types of research

- **Experimental methods:**
  - **Laboratory experiment:** an experiment that take places in a highly controlled, artificial environment, with an emphasis on removing all extraneous variables by using standardisation. The independent variable is manipulated by the researcher, and the dependent variable will be measured.
    - *High internal validity: takes place in a highly controlled environment so there is less likely to be extraneous variables which would reduce the validity of the experiment*
    - *Low mundane realism: the tasks are artificial and so how little resemblance to the real world where people may respond differently.*
  - **Field experiment:** an experiment that takes place in a naturalistic setting (e.g. a school, park, street) in contrast to the artificial environment of a lab study. The independent variable is still manipulated by the researcher.
    - *High ecological validity: takes place in a real-world setting, so behaviour is more likely to be natural.*
    - *Low internal validity: the researcher has little control over extraneous variables like the weather that may affect the study.*
  - **Quasi-experiment:** where the independent variable already exist in the individuals, so the participants can't be randomised between conditions. The aim of this method is to establish cause and effect.
    - *Lack of internal validity: difficult to isolate variables.*
    - *Confounding variables: individual differences may affect the research and become confounding variables*
  - **Natural experiment:** an experiment where the variable changes naturally without intervention from the researcher. The researcher uses this opportunity to study their topic.
    - *Low risk of demand characteristics: the researchers uses natural situations where people are acting as they would usually. This removes the risk of demand characteristics.*
- **Self-report techniques:**
  - **Questionnaires:** a standardised set of questions that all participants involved will answer. It can an either use open or closed questions. Open questions don't have a fixed set of responses and allows the participants to answer in their own way. Closed questions have a fixed set of responses such as yes/no questions or multiple-choice questions.
  - **Interviews:** where a participant is asked questions in person. They are either structured of unstructured. Structured interviews have a set, standardised list of questions that they will ask every participant in the same order. Unstructured interviews are not ordered and allow the participant to explore the topic at hand in their own way.
- **Observational techniques:**
  - **Naturalistic:** where the observer watches a real-life setting (e.g. watching a road and marking down how many people ride a bike vs. a car).
  - **Controlled:** observation is created in an artificial setting (e.g. Ainsworth's Strange Situation).
  - **Covert:** the participants aren't aware that they're being observed (e.g. researchers watching via hidden cameras or two-way mirrors).
  - **Overt:** the participants are aware that they're being observed (e.g. researchers sitting in the back of a classroom observing students).
  - **Participant:** the researcher is actively involved in the situation that they are observing (e.g. Zimbardo's prison experiment where he played the role of the police sergeant).
  - **Non-participant:** the researcher isn't actively involved in the situation that they are observing (e.g. Milgram's experiment where other people played the role of the experimenter and learner).
- **Content analysis:** used to analyse qualitative data and transform it into quantitative data. The form of data they used can be obtained through interview transcripts, diaries, audio recordings etc. To analyse it, they come up with coding units. This may be the number of times someone says a specific word.
    - *Reliable: researchers will apply the same coding units through time which makes this method replicable.*
    - *Cause and effect: it's hard to identify the cause and effect of information that is being analysed so it may lack depth*
- **Case studies:** in-depth forms of research that focus on studies of select individuals. These individuals usually have rare conditions or have been through unusual situations which lead researchers to want to analyse them.
    - *Reliable: in-depth, meaningful data is produced based on a lot of research on one person.*
    - *Lack generalisability: psychologists are usually unable to make broad assumptions based on a single person's situation.*

Scientific processes

- **Aim:** what the researchers are investigating and why. For example, in one of Asch's variations, his aim was to study the effects of social support on rate of compliance.
- **Hypothesis:** they aim to test a hypothesis. The hypothesis is what they predict will be the results of their study. The three different kinds of hypothesis are:
  - **Directional:** predicts the direction which the research will go in
  - **Non-directional:** predicts that there will be a difference between the variables but doesn't specify a direction.
  - **Null hypothesis:** prediction that there is no relationship between two variables
- **Sampling:**
  - **Population:** an entire group of people that the researcher wants to study for example all men, all teenagers, all UK adults.
  - **Sample:** a part a population which is representative of the entire population
  - **Sampling techniques:**
    - **Random sampling:** where the researcher selects a random sample of participants from a target population. This may be done by choosing names from a hat or from a random name generator. This method allows everyone to have a fair chance of being selected.
    - **Systematic sampling:** selects a sample of participants based on set intervals. For example, picking every 5th and 9th name from a list.
    - **Stratified sampling:** the researcher with split the population into different groups, working out what percentage of the population is in each group and then using random sampling to select names.
    - **Opportunity sampling:** the researcher will approach people that are available and ask them to take part in the study.
    - **Volunteer sampling:** this is where a researcher will put out an advertisement for volunteers, and people will sign up based on their own interest.
- **Pilot studies:** a form of practice research using a downscaled group and running through the procedure. The aim of a pilot study is to identify any areas for improvement in the study design before fully conducting the research. For example, if the task is too difficult, the participants may lose interest in the study and won't perform as the researcher desires. By detecting these issues, the researcher may be able to save time and money.
- **Experimental designs:**
  - **Repeated measures:** where participants will participate both research conditions. They'll complete task A, followed by task B and then the results are compared.
  - **Independent groups:** participants are divided into two groups and participate in separate conditions and then results are compared.
  - **Matched pairs/independent group design:** a group of participants are matched with another group of participants based on similar characteristics of the original group to try and control for those characteristics.
- **Observational design:**
  - **Behavioural categories:** the researcher curates a list of behaviours to observe and record. This allows the study to be replicable and for different observers to be consistent in what they are looking for. Behaviour will then be coded into these categories rather than being written descriptively.
  - **Event sampling:** this is where the researcher will record every time they observe a behaviour
  - **Time sampling:** this is where the researcher will record behaviour at select intervals of time
- **Variables:**
  - **Independent variable:** is something that is changed by the researcher.
  - **Dependent variable:** is the thing that is measured by the researcher.
  - **Extraneous variables:** unwanted variables that can lead to results of the experiment being skewed, which therefore leads to false conclusions being drawn.
  - **Confounding variable:** one that hasn't been properly controlled and has actually affected the results of the experiment (i.e. something other than the IV that has changed the DV).
  - **Operationalisation of variables:** where the researcher defines a variable in terms of the study which allows them to turn an abstract concept into something measurable. For example, if the dependent variable the researcher is studying is anxiety, they will need to find a way to measure the level of anxiety, such as by using a blood pressure monitor.

Scientific processes (continued)

- **Means of controlling experiments:**
  - **Random allocation:** this is where people are randomly assigned to a group which helps to remove any researcher bias
  - **Counter-balancing:** used to deal with order effects in a repeated measure design. Order effects refer to how completing tasks in a specific order may affect the research (e.g. if someone completes one task, they may already think they have figured out the aim, which may affect performance in the second condition). Half of the participants will complete the study in one order, and the other half will complete it in the other order so as to combat order effects.
  - **Randomisation:** where participants are randomly allocated to conditions in order to eliminate bias.
  - **Standardisation:** where the conditions and standards are kept the same for every participant.
  - **Control groups:** a group of people who don't take part in the experimental conditions and instead act as a group to compare the experimental group to.
- **Demand characteristics and investigator effects:**
  - **Demand characteristics:** extraneous variable where a participant acts according to how they think the researcher wants them to, reducing ecological validity.
  - **Investigator effects:** an extraneous variable where the characteristic of the researcher affects the participants' behaviour, leading to a reduction in ecological validity.
- **Ethics:** when research is ethically conducted, health and safety of the participants will be considered. The British Psychological Association code of ethics covers:
  - **Consent:** participants should be told the aims of the study, data being collected, and any possible risks of the study before giving their informed consent. They have the right to withdraw at any time. The researchers must consider the participants actual ability to consent e.g. mental stability or undue pressure.
  - **Deception:** researchers can't mislead participants about the nature of the study. But there are a few exceptions which require a level of deception (e.g. Asch's study wouldn't have provided valid results if participants knew the true nature of the study). It can be scientifically justified to have some degree of deception, so psychologists must use risk management to avoid harm:
    - **General consent:** telling the participants that they will be deceived without telling them how. This may affect the participants' behaviour.
    - **Retrospective consent:** telling the participants that they were deceived after the research and then asking for consent to use their data.
  - **Confidentiality:** personal data of participants cannot be disclosed. Any identifiable data cannot be published.
  - **Debriefing:** after the research has been conducted, researchers have to explain all details of the study to the participants. If a participant has been harmed in the study, the researched must address the harm so that the participant is in a stable state to leave.
- **Peer review:** assesses the scientific credibility of a research paper before it's published in a research journal. Researchers will submit their paper to the journal who sends it to an expert to evaluate its scientific validity, then accept, revise, or reject the paper. **Single-blind:** researchers don't know the name of the reviewers.
  - **Double-blind:** the researcher doesn't know the name of the reviewers and the reviewers don't know the name of the researcher.
  - **Open review:** the researchers and reviewers are both known to one another.
- **Economic implications of psychological research:**
  - Attachment research can inform policies like maternity/paternity leave to invest in the secure attachment of children and help them lead healthier, productive lives.
  - Memory research can inform criminology and the legal system, reducing wrongful conditions and saving money on appeals and prison costs.
  - Mental health research can inform our understanding of people's holistic health, particularly in preventative and best practice measures that reduce strain on the NHS and increases people's productivity in the long term.
- **Reliability:**
  - **Test-retest:** presenting the same participants with the same test on two separate occasions, then see if there is a positive correlation between the two.
  - **Inter-rater:** to what degree different psychologists give similar estimates.
  - **Inter-observer:** do independent observations of the same situation at the same time tally every time? Comparing results from different observers can establish a correlation – if the correlation is 0.8 or more, it's statistically significant.
- **Validity:**
  - **Temporal:** are findings permanent/relevant to date?
  - **Population:** can it be generalised to the whole population?
  - **Concurrent:** do the results match an already established test?
  - **Face:** does the test do what it says it's going to do?
  - **Internal:** does the study measure what it wants to?
  - **External:** can the results be generalised to other situations outside research environment?
  - **Construct:** does it successfully measure a concept it's supposed to?
  - **Ecological:** is it generalisable to the real world?
- **Features of science:**
  - **Objectivity:** observations made without judgement from a neutral perspective.
  - **Empirical method:** where research is carried out in a scientific manner based on empirical judgements.
  - **Reproducibility:** where experiments are replicated to ensure valid findings.
  - **Falsifiability:** when a hypothesis is tested there must be a possible observation that it can be proven false.
  - **Paradigm shifts:** science isn't fully objective and unbiased, nor does it always progress linearly. Most scientists accept exiting theories as true and then use these theories to find supporting research, but may need to adjust if theories are challenged. A paradigm shift is where we replace one pre-existing set of ideas with a new one.

Data handling and analysis

- **Reporting psychological investigations:** the features of a scientific report are:
  - **Title:** short description of the research.
  - **Abstract:** a summary of the research which includes a hypothesis, method(s), results and a conclusion.
  - **Introduction:** a broad overview of the context of the research. Then you focus on the particular study and mention its aims, hypothesis and why it was carried out.
  - **Method:** this is a detailed description of the procedure used in the study. This is so it can be evaluated by also replicated. It mentions: the study design (method used e.g. independent groups or repeated measures, operationalisation of variables), the participants (target population that was studied, sampling method and how many were used), equipment used (description of any specialised equipment and how it was used), standardised procedure (step-by-step description of how it was carried out) and controls (how extraneous variables were controlled).
  - **Results:** a summary of data and key findings collected from the research.
  - **Discussion:** explanation of results and how they relate to the experimental hypothesis. They address any issues that came up when conducting the research, suggestions for future research and how the results fit other research.
  - **Conclusion:** short summary of key findings.
  - **References:** a list of sources that may have been used in the study.
- **Types of data:**
  - **Quantitative data:** numerical data that is more objective, collected from techniques like closed-question questionnaires.
  - **Qualitative data:** not numerical and provides more insight into the individual's life, collected from techniques like open-ended interviews.
  - **Primary data:** the researcher collects the data first-hand, such as in an interview.
  - **Secondary data:** the researcher uses other data to draw own conclusions on their research (e.g. meta-analysis – a study of other studies that involves taking studies from the same research area and using it to identify trends to create a larger study).
- **Descriptive statistics:**
  - **Measures of central tendency:**
    - **Mean:** the average of a set of data, calculated by adding all numbers together and dividing by total amount of numbers.
    - **Median:** the middle result from a set of data, calculated by arranging all the numbers in a set from smallest to largest and then finding the middle number.
    - **Mode:** the most common figure, calculated by finding the most frequently occurring number in a set.
  - **Measures of dispersion:**
    - **Range:** the range from the smallest to largest number.
    - **Standard deviation:** how much numbers in the set deviate from the mean. To calculate, first find the mean, then subtract the mean from each number in the set and square these numbers. Add all of the numbers together and then divide the result by the number of numbers. The square root of these numbers is the standard deviation.
  - **Percentages change:** work out the difference between the original number and the other number, divide the difference by the original number, then multiply by 100.
- **Distribution:**
  - **Normal distribution**: is a symmetrical curve where the majority of the scores are on/near the mean average, and there is an equal number of scores above and below the mean.
  - **Skewed distribution:** an asymmetrical curve with an unequal distribution of scores either side of the mean. This shape is caused by anomalous results which lead the curve to skew either positively or negatively.
    - **Positive skew:** a high score makes the mean a lot higher than most of the scores which makes most scores below the mean (i.e. mean > median).
    - **Negative skew:** a low score makes the mean a lot lower than most of the scores which makes most below the mean (i.e. mean < median).
- **Correlation:** the relationship between two variables. They will either be closely related and have a positive correlation or be weakly related and have a negative correlation. Correlations are measured using correlation coefficients. These range between +1 and -1.
  - r=+1 means two things are perfectly correlated. One goes up, the other goes up by the same amount.
  - r=-1 means two things are negatively correlated. One goes down, the other goes down by the same amount.
  - r=0 means two things aren't correlated.
- **Levels of measurement:**
  - **Nominal data:** named data that can be separated into categories that do not overlap.
  - **Ordinal data:** placed into an order or scale.
  - **Interval data:** comes in a numerical form that is standardised.
- **Inferential testing:**
  - **Statistical testing – the sign test:** a way to calculate the statistical significance of differences between related pairs of nominal data. If the observed value is equal to or less than the critical value, then the results are statistically significant.
    - Look if your experimental hypothesis is two-tailed (a change is expected in either direction) or one-tailed (a change is expected to go in one direction).
    - Find the p value – this determines significance of a result.
    - Look for your critical value in a critical values table.
    - Calculate your observed value (count when the less frequent sign appears).
  - **Inferential tests:** how to decide which test to use:

	Test of difference		Test of correlation
	Related	Unrelated	
Nominal	Sign test	Chi squared	Chi squared
Ordinal	Mann Whitney	Wilcoxon	Spearman's Rho
Interval	Unrelated T test	Related T test	Pearson's R

- **Type 1 and type 2 errors:**
  - **Type 1 error – false positive:** where researchers decide an effect is real (reject the null hypothesis) but there is no effect.
  - **Type 2 – false negative:** where researchers decide there is no effect and accept the null hypothesis but there is a real effect.

Gender

- **Gender bias:** gender bias is a distorted view of behaviour which may be typical or atypical of either gender. This includes the different treatment of men and women that is based on stereotypes not factual information. Psychology has typically been male-dominated meaning the majority of its theories and approaches reflect only the male dominated perspective. The female voice has been minimised and judged as inferior to the male standard.
- **Androcentrism:** when something is male-centred. In psychology, it's when behaviour is judged based on male standards and may not adequately account for the broader population.
- **Alpha bias:** exaggerates the differences between men and women. This can devalue one gender compared to the other (usually men over women).
- **Beta bias:** when differences between men and women are downplayed. They assume that because one thing is true for one gender, it can be generalised to the other.
- **Universality:** characteristics of human beings can be generalised to all human beings. This is done by accepting real differences, but not making one superior to the other.
- **Evaluation of gender bias debates:**
  - ◆ *Evidence of bias: historically, most psychologists were men and the majority existing published research is by men. Therefore, female views may not be reflected in the research. These are forms of institutional sexism.*
  - ◆ *Reflexivity: researchers must reflect on any possible biases in their research and how it may have affected the outcome, leading to a greater awareness of biases.*
  - ◆ *Evidence of bias: having stereotypical assumptions based on biased research can have a damaging effect on the lives of women. It creates untrue, misleading assumptions about female behaviour that can lead to the validation of discrimination (e.g. lack of equality in the workplace has been justified by Bowlby's monotropic theory of attachment (see page 6) by arguing that women need to stay home and shouldn't work if they have children).*

Cultural bias

- **Universality:** the aspiration that psychological findings apply to all humans. However, this is frequently undermined by reliance on WEIRD (Western, Educated, Industrialised, Rich, Democratic) samples, raising issues with generalisability. The majority of psychological research and researchers have either been with American participants which makes it liable to WEIRD bias.
- **Ethnocentrism:** the belief that one's culture is superior to another. When you judge cultures by the same standard as your own culture (i.e. using an imposed etic) it can result in inappropriate research.
- **Etic approach:** looks at behaviour outside of the culture and it attempts to explain and identify behaviour as universal. This can raise issues with validity (e.g. using IQ tests that are subject to WEIRD bias to assess intelligence in another culture will result in invalid data).
- **Emic approach:** looks at behaviour within the culture and attempts to explain and identity behaviour specific to that culture. This approach advocates for understanding behaviour within its cultural context and resisting universal judgments.
- **Cultural relativism:** behaviour cannot be judged unless it is judged in the context of its culture.
- **Evaluation of cultural bias debates:**
  - ◆ *Identifying bias has led to a move towards more culturally sensitive research (e.g. indigenous psychologies, cross-cultural studies), reducing the risk of ethnocentrism and enhancing universality. However, some research risks treating all behaviours as equally valid, making it difficult to draw conclusions.*
  - ◆ *Western psychology still dominates academic publishing and theory-building, limiting global perspectives.*

Determinism and free will

- **Hard determinism:** argues free will is illusory. Behaviour is entirely shaped by identifiable causes, especially environmental factors in behaviorism. B.F. Skinner was a notable proponent, suggesting even moral choices are pre-determined.
- **Soft determinism (compatibilism):** accepts causal influences but maintains that humans have meaningful choice within constraints. Cognitive psychologists often adopt this middle ground; behaviour is influenced but not rigidly dictated.
- **Biological determinism:** behaviour is controlled by our genes, hormones, and neurochemistry.
- **Environmental determinism:** we may think that we are acting on free will, but all of our actions are constantly being determined by our environment and who we surround ourselves with.
- **Physic determinism:** behaviour is decided and directed by our unconscious thoughts (e.g. memories or repressed childhood experiences).
- **Evaluation of determinism and free will debates:**
  - ◆ *Consistent with the aims of science – everything has a cause and effect. Science can act as a predictor for human behaviour, based on things such as brain chemistry. For example, if someone lacks a certain amount of neurotransmitters, they are more likely to get depression.*
  - ◆ *The concept of free will has face validity as it aligns with normal experiences – every day, humans make conscious decisions about what to do.*
  - ◆ *Determinism isn't consistent with the legal system – people are held morally accountable for their actions in court. If all behaviour is determined, then there wouldn't be a reason to punish criminals for their actions, and there is no way to prevent recidivism.*

SNAPREVISE

Nature vs. nurture

- This debate is about the extent to which aspects of behaviour are as a result of inherited influences or environmental influences.
  - Nature: behaviour is innate.
  - Nurture: behaviour is learnt.
- For example, Locke argued that we have a 'blank slate' at birth and become who we are as a result of the environment we grow in.
- Previously, psychologists would argue either one side or the other, but now they're more concerned with the interaction between the two.
- **The interactionist approach:** nature and nurture interact with another. A child's innate temperament will change the way the parents respond to them, which affects the child's behaviour.
- **The diathesis-stress model:** models of mental illness that emphasis the interaction of nature and nurture. For example, psychopathy is caused by a genetic vulnerability but is expressed when combined with an environmental trigger.
- **The heritability coefficient:** used to assess heritability of characteristics. It ranges from 0-1 which explains the extent to which a characteristic has a genetic basis. 1 is completely genetic and 0 is environmental.
- **Evaluation of nature vs. nurture debates:**
  - ◆ *Most contemporary psychology adopts an interactionist stance (e.g. gene-environment interactions in epigenetics), making the debate more nuanced.*
  - ◆ *Extreme nature or nurture positions can be reductionist, oversimplifying complex human behaviour.*
  - ◆ *Understanding both sides informs therapies (e.g. biological treatments + behavioural interventions are often the most effective combination).*

Idiographic vs. nomothetic approach

- **The idiographic approach:** people are studied as unique individuals and there's no attempt to compare them to a norm or generalise behaviour. This is usually associated with qualitative research methods.
- **The nomothetic approach:** seek to establish a general law of human behaviour and compare everyone to that law in order to predict behaviour. This is usually associated with quantitative methods.
- **Evaluation of idiographic vs. nomothetic debates:**
  - ◆ *The idiographic approach produces rich meaningful data contrasting to nomothetic methods, but findings may lack generalisability.*
  - ◆ *Nomothetic approaches tend to be more scientific so can be used to establish laws about human behaviour, but may overlook individual differences leading to a 'one size fits all' mentality.*
  - ◆ *A combined approach is often most effective (i.e. idiographic insights alongside nomothetic generalisations).*

Holism and reductionism

- **Holism:** the idea that 'the whole is greater than the sum of its parts.' Any attempt to break up behaviour in psychology is inappropriate as they can only be understood by analysing the person as a whole.
- **Reductionism:** attempts to break actions and thoughts down to its smallest parts and dissect it. This is usually viewed as a scientific approach as it agrees that everything should be explained using basic principles.
- **Types of reductionism:**
  - **Biological reductionism:** based on the idea that we are biological organisms made up of structures. All behaviour is biological on some level.
  - **Environmental reductionism:** ignores any mental influences and focuses on how people are strictly influenced by environment.
- **Evaluation of holism and reductionism debates:**
  - ◆ *Holism captures the complexity of human experience but is often impractical for scientific testing since it can be too broad and vague to produce clear interventions that lead to practical applications.*
  - ◆ *Reductionism enables scientific analysis, experiments, and effective treatments (e.g. SSRIs for depression), but it can oversimplify individual experiences, ignore emergent research, and fail to account for under-researched concepts or under-represented cultural context (e.g. social/environmental influences).*

Social sensitivity in psychological research

- **Social sensitivity:** research on some topics in psychology may be controversial, especially if the results may stigmatise certain groups.
- This raises ethical concerns including privacy issues and misuse of findings. Researchers must be mindful of wording, context, and societal impact when exploring such topics.
- When researching, psychologists and scientists need to think about:
  - Their research question – ask the question carefully.
  - The methodology used – consider the treatment of individuals.
  - The motive behind the research – be mindful of how the results are going to be used.
- **Evaluation of social sensitivity debates:**
  - ◆ *Tackling sensitive topics (e.g. mental health, social prejudice) can raise awareness and promote social change.*
  - ◆ *Ethical frameworks: awareness of social sensitivity encourages more careful, responsible research design.*
  - ◆ *Participants or groups may face stereotyping, discrimination, or psychological harm.*
  - ◆ *Findings may be politically or socially exploited (e.g. research on race and gender differences).*

Options

Option 1

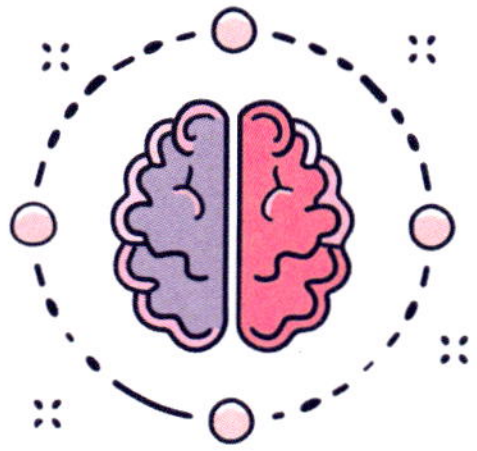

Option 2

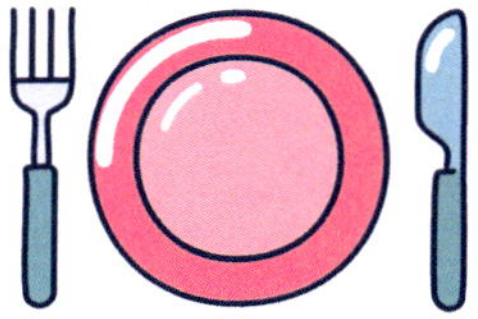

Option 3

Factors affecting attraction

- **Self-disclosure:** (**Jourard 1971**) when we get into a relationship, we are excited to learn about our new partner and reveal things to them about our fears, hopes, dreams, attitudes, and interests. You need three things for self-disclosure:
  - **Social penetration theory:** this is the process of revealing our inner self. It's important as it shows trust and commitment. As people share more sensitive information with their partners, they penetrate more deeply into each other's lives. This leads to a greater trust and a deeper understanding of each other.
  - **Breadth and depth:** the topics of conversation become broader as people trust each other, becoming deeper with more trust. If too much is shared too soon, the relationship may not last. Likewise, if too little is shared over time, the relationship is unlikely to last.
  - **Reciprocity of self-disclosure:** we will feel too vulnerable with our partner if self-disclosure isn't reciprocated.
- **Physical attractiveness:** there is an evolutionary explanation for why physical attractiveness is so important:
  - **Sexual selection:** reveal clues about our health and quality of genes. **Shackleford and Larson (1997)** found that people with symmetrical faces are seen as more attractive because it is a good signal of genetic fitness. People also tend to be attracted to 'baby faces' as they trigger a caring instinct in us. These ideas are universal across all cultures as humans want to find a genetically suitable partner.
  - **The Halo effect:** **Dion et al. (1972)** found that more physically attractive people are seen as kinder, smarter, stronger, and more successful. Children that were more conventionally attractive were seen as better behaved than less attractive ones. This is because physical attractiveness can create a metaphorical halo that makes us view someone in a more favourable light even when assessing unrelated traits like intelligence or empathy.
- **The matching hypothesis:** people are attracted to those seen as having a similar level of attractiveness to us. We first asses our own value and then attempt to find a partner with a similar attraction. Even if we are attracted to someone of 'higher' attractiveness, we will try to get a partner we view as in our league.
  - **Walster et al.'s (1966)** study challenged this by experimenting with 350 students attending a dance. 4 student judges were secretly selected to assess the student's level of attractiveness. They were randomly paired for the dance and then asked if they would like to see them again. This study didn't support the theory as everyone preferred the more attractive people, not their matched pair.
- **Filter theory:** **Kerchoff and Davis (1962)** outlined 3 main factors which filter our choice to a field of desirables:
  - **Social demography:** the range of factors that influence the chances of meeting our partner in the first place (e.g. location, schedule). We're more likely to meet people with a similar social demography to us as we like being around people who are socially and culturally homogenous to us.
  - **Similarity in attitudes:** values and attitudes are very important in early stages of a relationship as people want to agree on core values and are unlikely to pursue a relationship if there are huge discrepancies in attitudes. This helps to encourage self-disclosure in the early stages.
  - **Complementarity:** this is where partners fulfil each other's needs and complement/balance each other – one may have certain traits that the other doesn't. This factor is important in long-term relationships.

Theories of romantic relationships

- **The social exchange theory:** in relationships, there is a series of exchanges. We aim to maximise rewards and minimise costs/losses.
- The satisfaction of a relationship is reliant on the profitability of the relationship. Rewards and costs are subjective (e.g. money, sex, friendship, quality time).
  - **Comparison levels:** in a relationship we are judging whether our partner is living up to our expectations and the relationship provides what we expect it to. These expectations can be based on previous relationships, media influences, social norms, and how we view other relationships. It also depends on levels of self-esteem; for example, people with low self-esteem are more likely to stay in bad relationships and believe they don't deserve better.
  - **Comparison levels for alternatives:** assess if we are better off with someone else/alone. This is where we weigh up the potential increase in rewards with another partner and the potential costs if we leave our current partner. If we view a different person as better, we may leave our current partner.
- **Equity theory:** claims that the success of a relationship isn't based on rewards vs. cost, but on satisfaction and how equal partners feel within the relationship.
  - Equity is not the same as equality – partners don't need to gain the exact *same* rewards vs. costs but want to find a fair *balance* of rewards and costs. Equity leads to romantic satisfaction.

Theories of romantic relationships (continued)

- **Rusbult's (2001) investment model:** seen to be a development of social investment theory as it includes satisfaction and comparison of alternatives. This model stipulates that investment has a greater impact on comparison levels than satisfaction. It explains why dissatisfied partners choose to stay in a relationship that they have heavily invested in – they would rather choose to fix an unsatisfactory relationship they have spent time in rather than move on and feel like their time was wasted.
  - Satisfaction: high or low based on the comparison of rewards vs. costs.
  - Alternatives: other people we may deem as suitable partners if our partner isn't meeting our needs.
  - Investment: the level of time, money, and commitment put into a relationship.
- **Duck's (2007) phase model of relationship breakdown:** there are 4 main phases of a relationship breakdown:
  - **Intra-psychic:** this is where a person begins to feel dissatisfied in their relationship and spends a lot of time thinking about the reasons why. This is only internal – they do not share their feelings with their partner at this stage.
  - **Dyadic:** where the dissatisfied partner confronts their partner and initiates the break-up. There are typically many complaints from initiating partner. They also begin to look at alternatives and weigh up the costs vs. rewards.
  - **Social:** where both partners turn to their social groups in order to gain support in the break-up. There are many complaints to their friends, and it is hard for reconciliation to take place after this phase.
  - **Grave-dressing:** both partners create ideas of why the relationship broke down – often making themselves seem better and their partner appear worse. This signifies the end of a relationship and gives the person the feeling of needing to move on.

Online and parasocial relationships

- **Self-disclosure:** revealing personal information about ourselves. Anonymity that comes with online communication leads to people taking less accountability for their actions so there is a higher level of self-disclosure faster than in face-to-face relationships.
- **Gating:** obstacles that we use when we meet people face to face which determine if we let them further into our lives.
  - **The absence of gating:** (**McKenna and Bargh, 1999**) self-disclosure can happen without any distractions such as stammering or off-putting characteristics that can come across in face-to-face communication. Online, people are more interested in what is being said. They can also stretch the truth and create an identity that they wouldn't have in real life.
- **The reduced cues theory:** (**Sproull and Kisser, 1986**) online relationships are less effective than face to face relationships due to the lack of verbal cues present during communication which leads to a lack of trust. It leads to a lack of personal identity as de-individuation encourages disinhibition. This leads to blunt communication which reduces trust, and can lead to a lack of self-disclosure and consequently a lack of communication and connection.
- **The hyper-personal model:** (**Walther, 2011**) online relationships can actually become more intense more quickly than face to face relationships due to self-disclosure happening faster. People are able to skew their image online to seem more of an idealistic person. This is called selective self-presentation.
- **Levels of parasocial relationships:** **McCutcheon (2002)** identified three levels of parasocial relationships:
  - **Entertainment-social:** the least intense level. Celebrities are only viewed as forms of entertainment.
  - **Intense-personal:** the intermediate level. It reflects personal in a parasocial relationship with a celebrity.
  - **Borderline pathological:** the strongest level of a parasocial relationship. There is an over-identification with the celebrity and their life, culminating in fantasies or delusions.
- **The absorption-addiction model:** (**McCutcheon, 2002**) parasocial relationships tend to form due to a deficiency in someone's life. They may have low self-esteem, a weak sense of identity, or fail to develop fulfilling relationships in their own life. They use parasocial relationships as a way to escape reality. What may start as level one (entertainment-social) could turn into level three if triggered by a stressful event.
  - **Absorption:** seeking fulfilment in celebrity worship makes a person to turn their attention to over-identifying with a celebrity.
  - **Addiction:** they need to increase their closeness in order to gain satisfaction. This may lead to extreme behaviours or delusions.
- **The attachment theory explanation for parasocial relationships:** many psychologists claim this relationship links to attachment problems in childhood. Insecure resistant children are the most likely group to form parasocial relationships later in life.
- **Proximity seeking:** people want to be close to their attachment figure, so people seek out information about their celebrity which can exacerbate the parasocial relationship.
- **Secure base:** people get security from parasocial relationships as there is little risk of rejection.
- **Protest at separation:** will express anxiety at separation from attachment figure.

The role of chromosomes and hormones

- **Chromosomes:** strands of DNA containing many genes. These genes code for proteins and hormones.
- After fertilisation, the sperm and egg nuclei fuse to form a diploid cell, meaning it contains 46 chromosomes (a full set), arranged in 23 pairs. The genotype for females is **XX** and for males is **XY**. The Y chromosome is important as it differentiates whether the baby will be a male or a female.
- The Y chromosome triggers the activation of the SRY gene which triggers the production of androgens and directs the development of the testes which produce testosterone, an androgen (male hormone) that stimulates the production of male reproductive organs. High levels of **testosterone** are highly associated with higher levels of aggression. This is an evolutionary explanation. Higher levels of aggression have helped men retain their mates in the wild, which allowed their genes to be reproduced.
- **Oestrogen** is the female sex hormone. It triggers the development of the female reproductive system (ovaries, fallopian tubes, and vagina). Fluctuations in oestrogen (alongside progesterone) are associated with premenstrual symptoms, including mood changes.
- Women have higher levels of **oxytocin** than men. It is described as the 'love hormone' as it provides feelings of closeness and comfort. This may explain the stereotype that women are more caring than men. Oxytocin is also an evolved characteristic. Before and after birth, high concentrations of oxytocin are released into the mother's blood which facilitates bonding and stimulates uterine contractions and milk release.
- Having **atypical sex chromosome patterns** can cause Klinefelter's syndrome in males and Turner's syndrome in females.
    - Klinefelter syndrome is characterised by the genotype XXY and affects those who are biological males. People with this syndrome develop facial and physical features that are similar to females (e.g. softer faces) and gynecomastia (development of breasts which can lead to risk of breast cancer). Psychologically, people with this are more clumsy and score below average on tests of visuo-spatial and reading skills.
    - Turner's syndrome is when biological females only have one X chromosome instead of two. This means they only have 45 chromosomes and a genotype of XO. Females with this condition typically have short stature, underdeveloped secondary sexual characteristics, infertility, and no ovaries so do not have a menstrual cycle. Psychologically, people with Turner's have advanced reading skills but find social communication more challenging.

Cognitive explanations of gender development

- **Kohlberg's (1966) theory of gender constancy:** all children go through the same three stages of gender development:
    - **Gender identity:** occurs between ages 2 and 3 when a child can identify themselves as male or female. This is based on superficial characteristics and external appearances like hairstyle and clothing, so they may believe that if a person changes these characteristics, then their gender also changes.
    - **Gender stability:** occurs between ages 3 and 7 when a child can understand their own gender, and the fact that boys grow up to become men and girls grow up to become women.
    - **Gender constancy:** occurs from 7+ when a child understands that their gender and other people's genders are permanent concepts. This is typically when they want same-sex role models to imitate to confirm expectations of their behaviour.
    - **Munroe et al. (1984)** conducted research on children from Belize, Nepal, American Samoa, and Kenya and observed the same three stages, thus strengthening this theory.
- **Gender schema theory: Martin and Halverson (1981)** agreed with Kohlberg that there is a positive correlation between rising age and an increasingly sophisticated understanding of gender identity. However, they also suggested that there should be a higher emphasis on schemas as they theorised this was an active process, not a passive one.
    - Schemas are mental frameworks of preconceived ideas and beliefs about certain things. Martin and Halverson suggested a child begins to identify with a certain gender around the age of 2 to 3, then actively seek out information to confirm these ideas. This contrasts to Kohlberg as he believes that active gender-based behaviour imitation only begins after achieving gender constancy in stage 3.
    - The child's gender identity schema is likely to be based upon stereotypical male or female behaviours (e.g. girls doing dance and boys playing football). However, when the child's schema becomes more advanced with experience, they have higher self-esteem because they have confirmed their gender identity and had it validated by others.
    - With the development of children's gender identity schema comes the creation of in-groups and out-groups. Children will identify with their own in-group from the ages of 3 to 7 due to the higher self-esteem they gain from this, whereas after the age of 8 they will also gain an appreciation for the out-group.

Social learning explanation on gender development

- Social learning theory says that learning occurs through experience and can be learned either directly or indirectly. This process is carried out when children identify with a role model.
- This role model will someone usually be someone of the same sex who may be in a superior position to them (e.g. a teacher or a parent), though could also be identified through forms of media the child watches and seeks to replicate. This provides the child with expectations of how males and females should behave, though this may not lead to a positive outcome.
- Indirect learning takes place through vicarious reinforcement which increases the likelihood that the behaviour will be imitated.
- Differential reinforcement is a form of direct learning which is specific to gender development. Children will be rewarded by their parents or an agent of socialisation for displaying gender appropriate behaviours.
    - Vicarious reinforcement and indirect form of learning occurs when a child sees another same-sex child being rewarded for displaying gender appropriate behaviours. This same-sex child would become a role model, so the child wants to replicate their behaviour for the same reward.

Gender incongruence - biological and social explanations

- Gender incongruence develops when an individual believes their biological sex is not in line with their gender. Therefore, they experience gender dysphoria and identify with the opposite gender. The terms 'gender incongruence' and 'gender dysphoria' replaced the previous diagnostic label of 'gender identity disorder' in 2013 to reduce the stigma of the word 'disorder.'
- The cause for gender incongruence is not fully understood but is theorised to be a combination of biological and social factors. The treatment for gender incongruence involves socially transitioning (i.e. identifying as their preferred gender and having other people respect this) and may include hormone replacement therapy or gender-affirming surgeries.
- Genetic explanations have mainly focused on twin studies (e.g. **Coolidge (2002)** identified gender incongruence in 2.3% of 157 pairs of twins).
- Cognitive explanation: **Liben and Bigler (2002)** suggested that dual pathways occur when children acquire attitudes and behaviours that are in line with gender stereotypes. The personal pathways occurs when the child interests expresses an influence on traditional attitudes and behaviours. This causes them to change due to their rapidly changing schemas and what it means to be a male or female.

The influence of culture and media on gender roles

- **Mead (1935)** conducted cross cultural research which can provide useful insight into cultural differences in gender roles. She found that within the same island of New Guinea there were many differences in gender roles and temperaments of different tribes, challenging the idea that gender is biological.
- However there is also evidence of similarities between cultures concerning gender roles. **Munroe and Munroe (1975)** found that across cultures women and men had divided roles in the household; typically women wouldn't go to work and the men would be the breadwinner in the majority of the families that they researched.

The Bem Sex Role Inventory

- **Sandra Bem (1974)** developed the Bem Sex Role Inventory which consisted of 20 items that represented typically male characteristics, 20 typically female characteristics, and 20 neutral characteristics. She used self-report studies where participants would rate their own personality and then measured them for androgyny and masculinity.
- This is a self-report questionnaire so is subject to participants' biases and results may lack accuracy (e.g. people may have different understandings of what characteristics like 'leadership' mean and thus rank themselves differently).
- Self-esteem is a potential confounding variable as people with high self-esteem are more likely to rate themselves highly for stereotypically positive characteristics like 'confidence' and 'kindness').

Cognition and development

Piaget's theory of cognitive development

- **Piaget (1952)** suggested there were two types of learning: assimilation and accommodation.
  - **Assimilation** is when we are exposed to new information which does not completely change our existing knowledge so we assimilate it into an existing schema.
  - **Accommodation** is when we are exposed to new information which completely changes our existing knowledge and therefore to deal with this information, we accommodate it by forming a new schema.
  - The main difference between accommodation and assimilation is the creation of new schemas. Piaget suggested that when we are put in an unfamiliar situation and assimilation is not enough to understand it, we are in a state of **disequilibrium**. This means that we want to learn more about our environment improve our understanding of the new situation which can develop our schemas. This is called **equilibration**. Some schemas are innate (e.g. having reflex actions for grabbing) whereas some are more sophisticated with time which allows us to explore new situations.
- Evaluation for Piaget's research:
  - ◆ *Piaget only used a small sample of children who were predominantly white, middle class, and from well-educated families. Therefore, his research lacks representativity and ecological validity.*
  - ◆ *However, his research encouraged change in methods in education. He placed emphasis on the fact that learning is an active process, resulting in schools creating environments for children to explore (e.g. sensory sand pits). Additionally, it encouraged more project-based, hands-on learning projects to be implemented.*
- **Stages of development: Piaget (1971)** suggested there are key cognitive abilities which all children gain as they move through the 4 stages of intellectual development.
  1. **Sensorimotor stage (0-2 years old):** in this stage, infants explore the world around them using their senses and their movements – hence the term 'sensorimotor'. A key feature during this stage is the development of **object permanence**, which is the understanding that objects still exist even though the infant may not be able to see, feel, or hear them (e.g. knowing that their favourite toy doesn't disappear if their parent puts it in a toy box). Infants will also start to perform behaviours with a specific purpose in mind – this is called **goal-directed behaviour** (e.g. crawling over to the toy box in order to take out their favourite toy again).
  2. **Pre-operational stage (2-7 years old):** during this stage, young children are able to mentally imagine different objects and experiences. They will begin to increasingly use **symbolic thinking**, which is the ability to use words and pictures to represent things that aren't present. Piaget also believed that children in this stage tend to be egocentric and struggle to consider things from another's point of view. Often, children in this stage will use a type of thinking named **animism**, which is the belief that everything that exists has a consciousness. For example, they may worry that a broken toy may be 'hurt.' Another key cognitive accomplishment that occurs during this stage is **reversibility**, which is the ability to mentally follow a series of events back to the start (e.g. explaining the plot of a fairy tale from the happy ending back to the beginning).
  3. **Concrete operational stage (7-12 years old):** during this stage, the child can now perform true logical thought, and can accurately imagine the consequences of an action without actually performing the action. Children in this stage also understand the **conservation of mass** – that is, if something changes shape (e.g. pouring water from a tall glass into a wide one), its mass is still the same. Another key cognitive step is the understanding of **classification** (i.e. organising or separating objects into groups based on common features).
  4. **Formal operational stage (12+ years old):** during this stage, thought processes become more sophisticated. A key part of this is the use of **abstract thinking**, which involves being able to understand something without seeing, visualising, or experiencing it (which is required in the concrete operational stage). Children also further develop their ability to solve problems systematically, and develop **deductive reasoning skills** where they are able to combine multiple pieces of information to draw a conclusion (e.g. 1. If Bob catches the ball he wins. 2. Bob won. Therefore, Bob must have caught the ball). Finally, adolescents develop **idealistic thinking** which involves thinking about their (or others') most desirable characteristics, and try to be 'perfect.'

Vygotsky's theory of cognitive development

- **Vygotsky (1962)** theorised that learning was a social process where children gain new knowledge and reasoning skills from more advanced people seen as experts.
- He also saw language as a crucial cognitive skill which developed at an increased rate compared to other cognitive skills.
- He suggested that some aspects of knowledge and intelligence would only be acquired through certain interactions with experts. The knowledge is first **intermental** and then becomes **intramental** as the learner crosses the zone of proximal development.
- **The zone of proximal development:** the distance between the actual developmental level as determined by independent problem solving under adult guidance. To be able to cross the zone of proximal development, learners should receive help from more experienced peers for a process of scaffolding.
- **Scaffolding:** the kind of help the learner receives from the expert in an effort to cross into the zone of proximal development.
- This was a useful theory for education as it explained that even if a child was intelligent and eager to learn, there is still a limit to what they are capable of learning without sufficient support.

Baillargeon's explanation of infant abilities

- **Baillargeon (1985)** disagreed with Piaget, arguing that a child not searching for an object does not necessarily mean they lack object permanence, as other factors like limited attention could explain this.
- She developed the **violation of expectation method,** which shows that infants look longer at unexpected events, indicating surprise and a developing understanding of physical laws.
  - In her study with 24 infants aged 5–6 months, she tested object permanence using a tall and a short rabbit passing behind a screen with a window.
  - In the impossible condition, the tall rabbit should have been visible but was not, and infants looked significantly longer at this outcome, suggesting they expected the rabbit to reappear.
  - From this, Baillargeon concluded that infants as young as five months have object permanence.
- In later research **Baillargeon (2000)**, she explored containment (objects remain inside closed containers) and support (objects fall if unsupported but remain safe on stable surfaces).
  - She proposed the concept of a physical reasoning system, an innate ability that makes infants pay attention to unexpected events to strengthen their understanding of the physical world.

Development of social cognition

- **Selman's (1971) level of perspective talking:** perspective talking is the cognitive abilities take on the viewpoint or perspective of another person in both physical and social situations. Selman developed a series of stages each characterised by a fault in reasoning. He assessed 60 children using perspective taking tasks. This included the 'Holly and her kitten' task which presents children with a scenario of a child called Holly whose father makes her promise not to climb trees, then later finds a kitten stuck in a tree. The purpose of the task is to assess children's understanding of conflicting perspectives (e.g. Holly wants to help the kitten but doesn't want to make her father upset).
  - **Level 0: undifferentiated** (3–6 years old): children are socially egocentric and confuse their own feelings for others (e.g. a child saying 'Holly's father would be angry if she climbed the tree' without considering if her father might understand of her motivations).
  - **Level 1: socially informational** (6 to 8 years) where children can take on only a single perspective at each time (e.g. a child might say 'Holly's father would be angry because he doesn't know about the kitten').
  - **Level 2: self-reflective** (8 to 10 years) children can fully identify with and take on the viewpoint of another person but only identify with one perspective at a time (e.g. a child saying 'Holly might think her father will understand if she explains she is rescuing a kitten').
  - **Level 3: mutual role taking** (10 to 12 years) children can fully identify with and take on multiple perspective at a time (e.g. a child explaining both Holly and her father's points of view).
  - **Level 4: societal** (12+ years) children can now understand that social rules are needed to maintain order and taking on one person's perspective is not enough (e.g. a child saying 'Holly's father would approve of Holly knowing when it is okay to break rules for the greater good of helping others').
- **Social cognition: theory of mind and the Sally-Anne test:** theory of mind is the ability to understand what other people are thinking and feeling. **Baron-Cohen et al.'s (1985)** Sally-Anne test is a false belief task where participants are asked to identify where Sally would look for her marble after it had been moved without her knowledge. 80% of the control group (including 14 with Down syndrome and 27 neurotypical children) correctly answered, compared to 20% of the autistic group.
- **The mirror neuron system:**
  - Mirror neurons are a set of specialised neurons that are theorised to be located in the premotor cortex, the supplementary motor area, and the primary somatosensory cortex. These neurons are activated when we see the motor actions of others but are also activated when we perform motor actions ourselves.
  - There's a strong link between mirror neurons and understanding intention in others. **Gallese et al. (1996)** suggested that by identifying and reenacting the observed behaviours using our motor system, mirror neurons can then be used to understand the intentions behind actions. Understanding intention is a key part of perspective taking.
  - **Ramachadran (2000)** examined the role of mirror neurons in the development of humanity as a social species. He believed that the evolution of mirror neurons gave our ancestors evolutionary advantages by increasing likelihood of survival. Mirror neurons aided the learning of language and advanced practical skills (e.g. hunting and cooking).
  - **Oberman and Ramachadran (2006)** found that neurological deficits involving mirror neurons are a potential cause for an autistic spectrum disorder. If someone has a faulty mirror neuron system, they are unable to understand intention behind actions. This is referred to as the **broken mirror neuron hypothesis.** This may lead to an autistic person being more socially awkward as they struggle to read other people.
    - ◆ *Most of the research conducted into the mirror neuron hypothesis is purely correlational. Increase activity in one brain area while completing task is assumed to be mirror neurons; however, we cannot pinpoint it and can only indirectly study such phenomena. Some psychologists question whether mirror neurons even exist at all.*

Schizophrenia

Symptoms and co-morbidities

- When describing symptoms, the terms 'positive' and 'negative' are used in the mathematical sense of 'adding' and 'subtracting,' not good/bad.
- **Positive symptoms:** create a new behaviour (e.g. delusions and hallucinations).
- **Negative symptoms:** loss of an experience (e.g. speech poverty or avolition).
- **Delusions:** sets of belief with no basis on reality (e.g. believing that someone famous is stalking you).
- **Hallucinations:** a distorted perception of reality and real stimuli (e.g. hallucinating the voices of dead loved ones).
- **Speech poverty:** occurs when there's an abnormally low level of frequency and quality of speech.
- **Avolition:** sudden total loss of motivation and interest in self-initiated acts. It makes it harder to complete any regular, day-to-day tasks.
- **Co-morbidity:** high frequency of a diagnosis of two disorders together. There is a high co-morbidity of schizophrenia and other mental health disorders such as OCD.
- **Cultural bias:** research has shown that African-American men have a higher rate of schizophrenia diagnoses compared to the rates of white people. This could be attributed to cultural differences; for example, hearing voices would be viewed as a gift and a sign of increased connection to ancestors in African cultures. Additionally, psychiatrists may also have a racial bias against African-Americans, which increases the likelihood of false diagnosis.
- **Gender bias:** women are less likely to be diagnosed with schizophrenia. This is because women are better at masking their symptoms of Schizophrenia, or may distort the severity in order to appear more agreeable. The current diagnostic system doesn't account for this bias which increases the likelihood of an incorrect diagnosis.
- **Symptom overlap:** many symptoms of other conditions overlap with symptoms of schizophrenia, making it more difficult to diagnose. This can lead to inaccurate and missed diagnosis.

Biological explanations for schizophrenia

- **Gottesman (1991)** discovered a positive correlation between increasing genetic similarity of family members and their increased risk of developing schizophrenia.
  - He used family and twin studies to measure concordance rates: monozygotic twins – 48%, dizygotic twins – 17%, siblings – 9%, and parents 6%.
  - These results show a strong argument for the existence of candidate genes for schizophrenia. However, there is no 100% concordance rate, which shows that there is still an environmental influence for the development of schizophrenia.
- **Ripke (2014)** discovered that schizophrenia is a **polygenic** disorder (has multiple candidate genes which contribute to its development.) He used a broad sample of 5,000 cases of Swedish people with schizophrenia to establish this.
- **The dopamine hypothesis:** originally studies argued that hyperdopaminergia (too much dopamine) was responsible for schizophrenia, whereas it's now widely accepted that hypodopaminergia (not enough dopamine) is more likely to be responsible. The dopamine hypothesis has high practical applications for drug therapy like antipsychotics.
- **Neural correlates:** specific patterns of neural patterns coincide with specific psychological symptoms so it's assumed that they contribute towards the symptoms.

Psychological explanations for schizophrenia

- **Family dysfunction as a risk factor:** suggests that maladaptive family environments contribute to the development of schizophrenia. Key theories associated with this include the schizophrenogenic mother, double-bind communication, and expressed emotion (EE).
  - **Schizophrenogenic mother:** **Fromm-Reichmann (1948)** proposed that a cold, rejecting, and controlling mother fosters an environment of tension and mistrust. Lack of warmth and honesty in communication creates feelings of insecurity. This dysfunctional dynamic may lead to paranoid delusions as the child perceives others as hostile or untrustworthy.
  - **Double-bind theory:** **Bateson et al. (1956)** found that when children receive contradictory messages (e.g. verbal approval paired with hostile tone), these conflicting signals cause confusion about what is right or wrong, leaving the child unable to resolve the inconsistency. Expression of frustration or questioning unfairness is discouraged or punished, resulting in feelings of helplessness, anxiety, and delusional thinking as the child perceives the world as threatening and unpredictable.
  - **Expressed emotion:** refers to the critical, hostile, or over-involved attitudes displayed by family members towards a person with schizophrenia. Highly expressive environments increase stress and reduce the individual's ability to cope, leading to poorer treatment adherence (e.g. inconsistent medication use) and significantly higher risk of relapse.
- **Cognitive explanations – central control dysfunction:** schizophrenia is associated with impairments in cognitive processes, particularly central control (the ability to suppress automatic responses to perform deliberate actions). The Stroop Test illustrates this: patients struggle to name the ink colour of words that spell a different colour (e.g. the word 'red' printed in blue). This difficulty demonstrates cognitive derailment and inability to filter irrelevant information, contributing to disorganised thought and speech in schizophrenia.

Biological therapies for schizophrenia

- Antipsychotics are dopamine antagonists. They bind to complementary dopamine receptors on the postsynaptic membrane which prevents dopamine from binding. This has an inhibitory effect so there is a lower rate of action potential generation in the postsynaptic membrane and returns neurotransmission to a normal level. There are two types of antipsychotics that treat schizophrenia: typical and atypical.
  - **Typical antipsychotics:** first generation drugs (e.g. chlorpromazine) are calming sedatives that act on histamine receptors as well as dopamine receptors.
  - **Atypical antipsychotics:** second generation drugs to add to the effectiveness of first generation drugs and additionally help to reduce the side effects of the typical drugs. They target other neurotransmitter receptors (e.g. clozapine targets serotonin and glutamate receptors and helps improve cognitive functioning and mood).

Psychological therapies for schizophrenia

- There are two main therapies for schizophrenia: CBT and family therapy.
- **CBT:** attempts to rewire the schizophrenia patients' thinking. The therapist aims to understand their behaviour which helps them provide the best support and treatment for the specific patient. It can't cure schizophrenia, but patients gain comfort in understanding the cause of their symptoms - especially positive symptoms such as delusions and hallucinations. It aims to increase self-awareness and understand that they are not 'weird' for having such thoughts.
- **Family therapy:** the schizophrenia patient's family attends regular therapy sessions. It aims to reduce the stress of living with someone who has schizophrenia. The family learns how to detect the beginning of a psychotic episode and how to support their family member through it. The stress on the patient weakens, and it becomes more about co-operation.

The interactionist approach

- This approach unites both psychological and biological explanations. It observes how therapies should incorporate both biological and psychological factors of schizophrenia.
- **The diathesis-stress model:** theorises that schizophrenia may be biological in nature but is expressed by the environment. This idea has been applied to schizophrenia treatments where they aim to treat both the biological and physiological aspects of the condition.

The physiology of stress

- **Selye (1936):** developed the idea of the **general adaptation syndrome** which explains how stress helps us to adapt new situations through three stages.

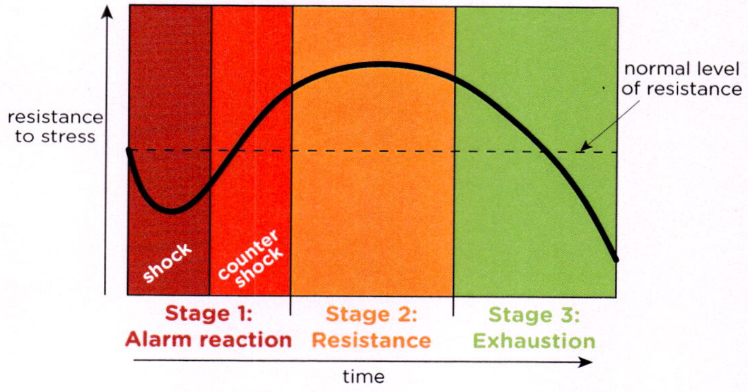

  - **Alarm:** describes immediate physiological response we experience upon seeing a stressor.
  - **Resistance:** in a situation of short-term stress, the body will try to resist the stressor through quickly using its energy resources. When the stressor becomes more permanent, increased activity is triggered in the parasympathetic branch in order to reduce physiological responses increased by the sympathetic branch.
  - **Exhaustion:** is where the original physiological symptoms come back and there is no energy left in the body this results in immunosuppression.
- There are two physiological responses to stress: acute and chronic.
  - **Acute response:** the body perceives an immediate stressor. This information is then passed through sensory neurons to the hypothalamus. The hypothalamus triggers a high level of activity in the sympathetic branch of the ANS. This produces the physiological changes needed to maintain the fight or flight response. When this dresser is gone increased activity in the parasympathetic branch decreases the activity which had been increased.
  - **Chronic response:** this is the activation of the hypothalamic pituitary adrenal system. It produces longer lasting effects compared to the hypothalamus. The release of corticotropin-releasing factor (CRF) results in higher activity of the pituitary gland which triggers the release of stress hormones. Cortisol creates the same fight or flight response but is a longer lasting reaction than the acute response.
  - ◆ *Beta bias: the majority of research into these physiological changes was completed on male mice. The reaction was generalised to females; however, newer research is showing that women have a different response to the fight or flight response.* **Taylor (2000)** *suggests that women have a tendency to 'tend-and-befriend' instead of 'fight-or-flight' in response to a stressor.*

The role of stress in illness

- The continuous release of **cortisol** from the **hypothalamic-pituitary-adrenal (HPA)** axis leads to immunosuppression. This can be either directly or indirectly by affecting other life factors which increase the risk of falling ill.

HPA axis

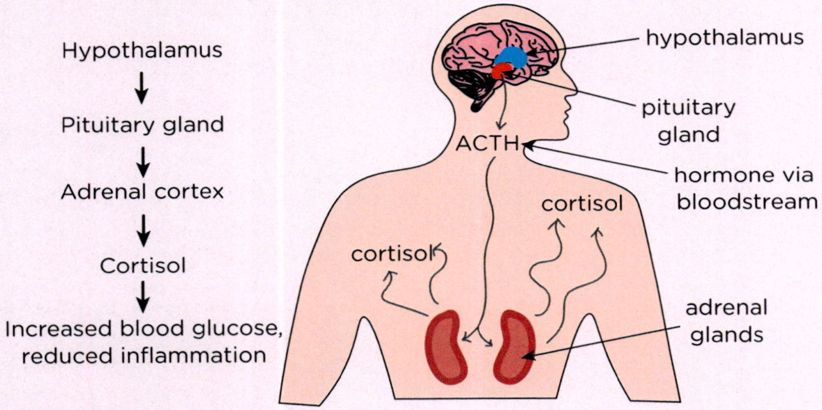

- Research into the reduction of natural killer cells anti killer cells in blood samples of medical students during exams compared to a month before their exams showed that students were more likely to get ill during the exam period due to increased stress.
- **Wilbert-Lampen (2008)** reported a 2.66 increase in the likelihood of suffering from an illness during the 2006 World Cup. Due to the stress on their bodies of performing in a world championship they were more likely to be subject to a myocardial infraction. Chronic stress may therefore be considered a more serious risk in the development of a myocardial infarction than obesity.
  - ◆ *Acute stresses could have a positive effect on health compared to chronic stresses. For example, some research has found that exposing rats to an acute stressor benefited the immune functioning of rats, meaning that the stress had an immunoenhancing effect. Hence, not all stress can be generalised to be bad for our health.*

Sources of stress

- **Life changes:** any life changes positive or negative can be stressful as they require adaptations which are supported by stress. Therefore, it's hard to judge if there is a positive correlation between an increasing extent of adaptation required and the increasingly high level of stress associated with life change.
  - Stress associated with life changes can be quantitatively measured using the social readjustment rating scale. Every stressful event is given a different life change unit (LCU). **Holmes and Rahe (1967)** found a positive correlation between increasing LCU and increasing likelihood of developing an illness.
  - In **Rahe's (1970)** double blind study found a positive correlation between Navy personnel who had experienced highly stressful life events six months before deployment and a higher likelihood of illness during their deployment.
    - ◆ *Ignores individual differences: we can't make universal assumptions based on people's life events as they're subjective. For example, a teenager moving out of home may be a negative life event for some, but if their household was abusive then it is a positive life event which actually alleviate stress.*
    - ◆ *Cause and effect: all studies of life changes are correlational. There is no cause and effect relationship, so it's difficult to draw conclusions based on this research, decreasing its external validity.*
- **Daily hassles:** are predictable, everyday occurrences that can be a proximal cause of stress as they indirectly result in a stress response, especially if they are unaddressed for a long time. **Lazarus and Folkman (1984)** suggested that each time we experienced daily hassle we go through two processes: assessing the severity of a hassle, and considering how to cope.
- **Workplace stress:**
  - Workload and control are the 2 main factors associated with workplace stress. This was theorised by the **job demand-control model** which suggests that the degree of control that an individual has over their work is more important than the workload in terms of determining stress levels. If two people have the same workload and one person is less stressed than the other, this means they have a higher degree of control over their work.
  - **Bosma (1997)** found no correlation between stress related illnesses and workload in a sample of 10,000 civil servants but a strong negative correlation between a decreasing degree of control over work and increasing levels of stress.
  - **Johansson at al. (1988)** found that workers who had little control over their work had higher levels of adrenaline in their urine samples compared to those in the same factory who had high control over their work. The concentrations of the hormones increase throughout the day, with increasing rates of stress-related illnesses.

Measuring stress

- The two widely regarded self-report measures of stress are the **social readjustment rating scale (SRRS)** and the hassles and uplift scale.
  - The SRRS is made-up of 43 items that are ranked on a scale of 1 to 43 with 1 being the most stressful and 43 being the least. Each item represents a stressful life event which is assigned an LCU based on **Holmes and Rahe's (1967)** research.
  - **The hassles and uplift scale** was developed by **Kanner et al. (1981)** and is made up of 117 items all ranked at different levels of causing stress. The severity was measured on a three-point like it like scale. The uplift scale uses the same mythology as the SSRS but uses positive stress reducing events (e.g. getting enough sleep, getting along with your work colleagues).
- Another measure of physiological stress would be the use of a **skin conductance response.** This is where electrodes are attached to the index and middle fingers and it detects an increase of sweat and how it links to an increase in conductance which produces readings on a polygraph against a baseline measure of no stress.

Individual differences in stress

- **Personality type:** research suggests that certain personality types are associated with an increased risk of developing certain illnesses such as coronary heart disease.
  - Type A personality: display traits like hostility and competitiveness that are positively correlated with developing coronary heart disease. **Friedman and Rosenman (1974)** suggested that people with Type A personalities were particularly vulnerable to stresses due to their intense personality. 70% of the 3000 males studied had Type A personalities and had developed coronary heart disease. This contrast to the type B personality who is usually viewed as more easygoing.
  - **Temoshok (1987)** theorised a type C personality which is heavily linked to developing depression. They are keen to please others but do so by suppressing their own emotions and feelings.
- **Hardiness:** has been defined by having resilience and adaptability to unexpected changes in our everyday lives. Hardiness can be measured according to an individual's level of commitment challenge and control.
  - **Kobasa (1979)** found significant differences in the effectiveness of managers and their ability to cope with stress in a sample of 670 American male managers. Those who seemed to cope well with stress also had high resilience which suggests that hardiness helps individuals cope with stress.
  - Research from **Maddi (1975)** found that out of 400 managers in the Bell Telephone Company during a period of reorganisation, there was a significant increase in the incident rates of stress related illness (e.g. coronary heart disease). Those who showed improved productivity and resilience had a decreased likelihood of developing stress related illnesses.

Managing and coping with stress

- **Stress inoculation therapy:** based on the theory that by changing the way we think about stress, we can decrease negative and irrational thinking by implementing more effective positive behaviours. Research suggests patients need to go through 3 stages:
  - **Conceptualisation phase:** a therapist will go through the patient's stresses with them, focusing on minimising the sources of stress that they can change while coming up with coping mechanisms for stress that is out of their control. This is an opportunity to give the patient a positive view of stress management.
  - **Skills acquisition and the rehearsal phase:** targets the cognitive aspects of stress; the therapist will teach the patient stress management skills (e.g. breathing techniques).
  - **Real-life application and follow-through phase:** the patient is forced to put their skills into practice (e.g. through role play or VR experiences). The therapist will suggest personal experiments where the patient deliberately puts themselves in stress-inducing situations to test the skills they have learned. If a patient relapses, it is acknowledged and accepted as an opportunity to further the skills of inoculation.
- **Biofeedback:**
  - **Budzynski (1973)** found patients can learn to identify, modify, and transfer changes to their physiological responses to stressors. Patients recognised their physiological responses through an auditory or visual sign and could train themselves to adjust their output such as reducing breathing rate to lowering the signal back to the normal baseline level through the process of biofeedback.
  - **Davis (1986)** found that urinary cortisol levels of in a sample of breast cancer patients undergoing weekly stress inoculation therapy sessions was significantly lower than a control group who experienced an increase in cortisol levels. This demonstrates that the therapy can be effective in lowering stress through the stabilisation of the HPA system and that can be achieved through biofeedback and operant conditioning.
- **Gender differences:**
  - The main difference between the genders with coping with stress is that men tend to take on a problem-solving, logical response whereas women are more likely to take an emotional response.
  - **Lazarus and Folkman (1984)** found the male approach tackles the cause of stress head-on whereas women tended to tackle the proximal causes of stress and associated stresses. They also found women tended to distract themselves from the stress and keep busy as a means of coping.
  - **Peterson (2003)** demonstrated this difference in relation to infertile males and females. He used a self-report study and found that men used practical solutions to alleviate the stressor whereas women more often accepted the blame and avoided directly addressing the stressor.
  - This is supported by **Taylor's (2000)** research into the fight or flight response. She postulated that women were more likely to use a 'tend and befriend' when faced with a stressor that meant they relied on social networks with other women who can relate and provide emotional support. This is the alternative to the fight or flight response which women are more likely to use.

Eating behaviour

SNAPREVISE

Explanations for food preferences

- **Evolutionary explanation:** humans evolved food preferences that increased survival chances.
  - Sweet foods are high in energy which made them highly valuable for hunter-gatherers (**Buss, 1998**), salt is essential for cell functioning and hydration balance, and fat-rich foods are calorie-dense, making them vital during food scarcity (**Cordain et al., 2000**).
  - **Neophobia:** reluctance to try new foods protects against poisoning. **Birch (1999)** found it most strong in early childhood when children are more vulnerable.
  - **Taste aversion:** adaptive mechanism to avoid harmful foods after illness. **Garcia and Koelling (1966)** demonstrated this in rats who developed an aversion to sweetened water after it had been paired with nausea, showing a biological preparedness to associate taste with sickness, which would have reduced the risk of consuming toxic foods.
    - ◆ *This explanation can be criticised as reductionist because while it explains universal preferences, it neglects the significant role of culture and learning.*
    - ◆ *In modern contexts, these once adaptive preferences for sweet and fatty foods may now be maladaptive, contributing to rising obesity rates – an example of 'evolutionary mismatch.'*
- **Role of learning:**
  - **Social influences:** research shows that social influences are crucial: parents shape their children's food habits both through modelling their own diets and through reinforcement (**Birch, 1980**). For example, if a parent consistently eats vegetables and praises the child for doing so, the child is more likely to develop a preference for them. Peer influences also become important in adolescence when conformity to friends' eating habits is strong.
  - **Cultural influences:** also shape food preferences by determining which foods are available and socially acceptable. **Rozin (1988)** found that cultural norms influence not only which foods are eaten, but also attitudes toward them. Additionally, exposure to global media has been shown to increase desire for high-calorie 'Western' diets, particularly among young people (MacIntyre et al., 1998).
    - ◆ *Unlike the evolutionary explanation, this learning-based account successfully explains cultural differences in diet. However, it may underestimate the role of biological predispositions, such as the universal preference for sweetness, suggesting that a full explanation must consider both innate and learned influences.*
    - ◆ *It is hard to separate social from biological influences since they both interact.*

Neural and hormonal mechanisms in eating behaviour

- **Hypothalamus:** eating behaviour is regulated by the brain, particularly the hypothalamus, which monitors blood glucose levels and hormonal signals related to hunger and satiety.
  - **Lateral hypothalamus (LH):** "hunger centre" stimulates eating when glucose levels drop.
  - **Ventromedial hypothalamus (VMH):** "satiety centre" signals to stop eating.
  - **Hetherington and Ranson (1942)** found that lesions to the VMH in rats led to continuous overeating and obesity, while damage to the LH caused anorexia. This suggests that different regions of the hypothalamus work in balance to regulate food intake.
  - However, **Gold (1973)** argued that eating behaviour cannot be explained by a simple dual-centre model, as other brain regions also play a role, making the process more complex than originally thought.
- **Hormones:**
  - **Ghrelin:** released from the stomach when it is empty, stimulates hunger by signalling the hypothalamus; ghrelin levels rise before meals and fall afterwards.
  - **Leptin:** produced by fat cells, suppresses appetite by signalling satiety. Deficiencies in leptin have been linked to obesity, and **Licinio et al. (2004)** reported that individuals with rare mutations in the leptin gene could be successfully treated with leptin therapy, reducing overeating, demonstrating the strong biological regulation of eating.
  - ◆ *Hormonal and neural explanations are somewhat reductionist since they neglect psychological and cultural influences on eating, such as stress or social norms, suggesting eating behaviour is best understood as an interaction between biology and environment.*

Biological explanations for anorexia nervosa

- **Genetic factors:**
  - Twin studies show higher concordance in identical twins, suggesting a hereditary component to anorexia nervosa. **Holland et al. (1988)** found concordance rates of 56% for identical twins compared to 5% for non-identical twins.
  - More recent studies have linked AN to particular genes affecting serotonin and dopamine functioning (**Kaye et al., 2001**), which are neurotransmitters involved in mood regulation and appetite control. Such findings suggest that individuals may inherit a predisposition to anorexia. However, concordance is far from 100%, indicating that environmental influences must also play a role.
- **Neural factors:**
  - Serotonin dysregulation has been associated with the anxiety and appetite suppression seen in anorexia nervosa. **Bailer et al. (2011)** found evidence of altered serotonin activity in anorexic patients even after recovery.
  - Dopamine abnormalities may contribute to a reduced sense of reward from food, explaining why individuals with anorexia nervosa derive little pleasure from eating.
  - Brain imaging studies show abnormal hypothalamic activity in anorexia patients, though this may reflect the consequences of starvation rather than its cause. Thus, biological explanations are valuable but incomplete, as they do not account for cultural influences.

Psychological explanations for anorexia nervosa

- **The family systems theory** (**Minuchin, 1978**) emphasises the role of dysfunctional family dynamics in the development of anorexia nervosa.
  - Families of anorexic individuals are often described as enmeshed, meaning that boundaries are blurred and individual autonomy is limited. These families also display overprotectiveness, rigidity, and conflict avoidance, which can create an environment where a young person feels powerless. Anorexia may thus be an attempt to assert autonomy and control.
  - **Bruch (1973)** supported this theory by finding that anorexia often arises in contexts where independence is suppressed. However, this theory has been criticised for gender bias, since it tends to blame mothers disproportionately for family dysfunction, and for failing to establish clear causality, as family difficulties may be the result rather than the cause of anorexia.
- **The social learning theory** proposes that anorexia nervosa develops through processes of modelling and reinforcement.
  - Individuals may observe peers, family members, or media figures who promote thinness and dieting, and imitate this behaviour. They may also be positively reinforced by praise for weight loss or thin appearance.
  - **Becker et al. (2002)** found that Fijian girls developed increased eating disorders after the introduction of television, demonstrating the powerful influence of media. However, not all individuals exposed to thin-ideal media develop anorexia, suggesting that individual differences moderate the effects of social learning.
- **Cognitive theories** argue that anorexia is maintained by faulty thought processes.
  - According to **Garner and Bemis (1982)**, anorexic individuals hold irrational beliefs and cognitive distortions, such as perceiving themselves as overweight despite being underweight, or believing that thinness equates to worth and success.
  - **Vitousek and Orimoto (1993)** found that anorexia nervosa patients often misperceive body size and display perfectionist thinking. These distortions can perpetuate the disorder even when weight loss becomes extreme.
  - The cognitive explanation is supported by the persistence of such beliefs in recovered patients, but critics argue that these thought patterns may be a consequence of starvation rather than a primary cause. Nevertheless, cognitive theories have informed effective therapies, such as cognitive behavioural therapy (CBT), giving them strong practical application.

Biological explanations for obesity

- Obesity has been linked to both **genetic and neural factors**.
- **Genetic research** has shown a strong heritable component. **Stunkard et al. (1990)** found that the heritability of body mass index (BMI) can be as high as 70%, and the FTO gene has been identified as increasing susceptibility to obesity. Such findings explain why obesity runs in families.
  - ◆ *However, genes alone cannot explain the rapid rise in global obesity, suggesting that environmental factors such as sedentary lifestyles and processed foods also play a major role. Thus, genes may create a predisposition, but do not determine outcomes.*
- **Neural explanations** highlight the role of hormones such as leptin and ghrelin. Individuals with leptin deficiencies fail to experience satiety and therefore overeat, while persistently high levels of ghrelin can cause ongoing hunger.
- Research has shown that leptin therapy can reduce obesity in individuals with rare leptin gene mutations (**Licinio et al., 2004**).
- The hypothalamus, which regulates hunger and satiety, is also implicated in obesity when functioning abnormally.
  - ◆ *While these biological findings are robust, they have been criticised as reductionist, because they downplay psychological factors such as stress eating and the influence of external food cues.*

Psychological explanations for obesity

- Psychological explanations emphasise the paradoxical effects of dieting and cognitive restraint.
- According to **restraint theory** (**Herman and Mack, 1975**), dieters deliberately restrict their food intake, but this often leads to overeating, particularly when self-control is disrupted. **Wardle and Beales (1988)** supported this by showing that dieters ate more than non-dieters when under stress. The disinhibition hypothesis further explains that individuals often lose control in response to emotional distress, alcohol consumption, or exposure to forbidden foods, leading to binge episodes.
- **The boundary model** (**Herman and Polivy, 1984**) expands on this by suggesting that hunger and satiety create biological boundaries for eating. In normal eaters, these boundaries prevent overeating. However, dieters extend their boundaries cognitively, making it easier to override satiety signals. Once the diet boundary is broken (e.g. through eating a forbidden food), overeating continues until extreme fullness is reached.
- These psychological theories are supported by experimental and observational research, and they explain why dieting is often unsuccessful and even counterproductive. However, they do not account for biological predispositions, and not all dieters become obese, which means these explanations may only apply to certain individuals.

Neural and hormonal mechanisms in aggression

- There are two types of aggression: **proactive aggression:** when someone deliberately plans to hurt someone to get what they want (e.g. premeditated murder), and **reactive aggression:** unplanned, impulsive aggression when people are angry (e.g. road rage).
- **Neural mechanisms:** the limbic system contains multiple components, including parts of the hippocampus, the hypothalamus, and the amygdala. The amygdala has a key role in how humans and animals assess and respond to environmental threats. The reactivity of the amygdala has been shown to be a good predictor of aggressive behaviour.
  - **Gospic's (2011)** lab study used fMRI scans to measure brain activity during a game called the Ultimatum game between two players where one is the prosperor and one is the responder. The prosperor offers to split money with the responder. If the responder rejects the offer, then they both get nothing. The results showed heightened arousal in the amygdala when the offer was rejected, suggesting aggression.
- **The role of serotonin:**
  - Serotonin is a neurotransmitter that regulates mood and is involved in the communication of impulses between the neurons. It has an inhibitory effect on the brain as it slows and dampens neural activity. Low levels of serotonin reduce self-control and increase impulsivity. Drugs that increase serotonin levels have been shown to reduce aggression.
  - In recent studies it's been shown that the amygdala functions alongside orbitofrontal cortex, not in isolation. This isn't involved in the limbic system, but plays a role in regulating mood and self-control. Therefore, the regulation of the amygdala is highly complex and can't just be put down to the amygdala alone.
  - **Virkkunen (1990)** examined the breakdown products of serotonin in criminals' cerebrospinal fluid. He compared violent, impulsive criminals to violent, non-impulsive criminals and found that the levels were significantly lower in impulsive criminals
- **Hormonal mechanisms in aggression:**
  - Testosterone is the male sex hormone and plays a role in regulating social behaviour. Generally, males tend to be more generally aggressive, and animal studies have shown a link between an increase in testosterone and a rise in aggression.
  - **Dolan (2001)** found a positive correlation between testosterone levels and aggressive behaviour in 60 male serious offenders in high security prisons in the UK.
- **Genetic factors:**
  - **Twin studies**: suggest that heritability is responsible for about 50 % of the variance in aggression. **Coccaro (1997)** found concordance rates of 50 % for MZ twins and 19% for DZ twins regarding physically aggressive behaviour. The figures for verbal aggression were 28% for MZ twins and 7% for DZ twins. However, a problem with using twin studies is that their behaviour may be influence by their environment.
  - **The MAOA gene:** MAOA is an enzyme that aids in recycling serotonin by mopping up leftover neurotransmitters after a nerve impulse, breaking down serotonin to be cycled or excreted. People who have dysfunctional MAOA genes have abnormal serotonin levels (i.e. low enzyme = low serotonin = impulsive behaviour and aggression).
  - This is supported by **Brunner (1993)** who studied 28 male members of a Dutch family who were consistently involved in violent and aggressive behaviour and found that each had low levels of the MAOA enzyme in their brain. **Stuart (2014)** also studied 97 men who had been convicted of domestic violence and found the men who committed the most violent abuse had the low activity version of the MAOA gene.

The ethological explanation of aggression

- Aggression is adaptive and offers animals survival advantages:
  - **Territory and resources**: this includes food, a water source, and mating opportunities to expand their population. This is adaptive and innate.
  - **Dominance hierarchies:** when male animals are higher up in this hierarchy, they get more mating opportunities.
- **Ritualistic aggression:** **Lorenz (1966)** observed fights between two animals of the same species. It rarely results in violence or death – the rituals usually end in submission by one of the animals to end the fight before any damage is done. It prevents the species from killing too many of its own population, which could end in extinction.
- **Innate releasing mechanisms and fixed action patterns:** an innate releasing mechanism is a built in physiological structure or process. An environmental stimulus triggers the IRM which releases a specific sequence of behaviours called a **fixed action pattern (FAP)** where each behaviour:
  - Is an adaptation (i.e. a hard-wired behaviour)
  - Must continue to completion once initiated
  - Cannot be changed
  - Is found throughout the species
  - Occurs as a response to a specific external stimulus known as a releaser
- **Tinbergen (2021)** observed that male stickleback fish get a red underbelly during mating season. If another male enters their territory, their FAP is triggered by seeing the red spot. He tested this by presenting male sticklebacks with wooden models that had red bellies. He found that regardless of the shape of the model, once the fish saw the red underbelly, the fish would display aggressive behaviour. If there wasn't a red belly, even if the model was in a fish shape, there was no response. He discovered that the FAP always ran its course.
- **Evolutionary explanations of aggression:**
  - Sexual jealousy is a major motivator for aggression in males. It's said to be a psychological mechanism that has adapted to encourage vigilance against cuckoldry and promote mate retention.
  - Mate retention strategies have evolved over time, including direct guarding and negative inducements. An example of direct guarding is constantly needing to know where your partner is and an example of negative inducements is threatening to kill yourself if your partner leaves you.
  - **Shackleford et al. (2005)** researched 107 married couples who had been married for less than year and used the mate retention inventory and spouses influence report, finding a positive correlation between marriage and aggressive behaviour.
  - Bullying confers an evolutionary advantage as men who bully other men are more likely to pass down their genes to as many offspring as possible. Female bullying is more likely to occur in relationships to ensure fidelity.

Social psychological explanations of aggression

- **Frustration-aggression hypothesis:**
  - **Dollard (1939)** proposed that frustration is a psychological reaction that always leads to aggression which is a product of frustration.
  - **Geen et al. (1977)** studied male university students undertaking tasks under 3 conditions. In one condition, the participants were being insulted whilst administering shocks. He found that those who found the puzzle the hardest gave the weakest shocks, those who were insulted gave the strongest shocks, and the lowest levels of frustration being displaced onto the control group. This supports his hypothesis as he argued that frustration is displaced onto other people when it can't be reduced.
  - **Berkowitz (1973)** didn't agree with the cathartic view, instead believing that frustration prepared people for aggression and that there were specific environmental cues that triggered this reaction.
- **Social learning theory:**
  - **Bandura's (1961)** Bobo doll experiment postulated that learning is a social process that occurs through imitation of certain behaviours. It can occur directly or indirectly (vicarious reinforcement).
  - Vicarious reinforcement occurs when we see a role model being rewarded for a certain behaviour. The observer is likely to replicate this modelled behaviour as they want to get the same reward.
  - Role models are those who have desirable characteristics, are often the same sex and of higher social status.
- **De-individuation :**
  - **Le Bon (1895)** proposed that deindividuation occurs as part of group behaviour where we feel no personal responsibility for our behaviour as the responsibility is shared within the group. We also aren't scared of retaliation in this setting as we view ourselves as an anonymous face amongst a crowd.
  - **Zimbardo (1969)** theorised that when we are in a crowd, our behaviour starts to stray from social norms and becomes disinhibited. Laws and social norms no longer apply to our behaviour because we can't be judged and are 'anonymous'.
  - Consequences of anonymity allow us to develop private self-awareness or public self-awareness.
    - Private self-awareness: we become less aware of our own beliefs as the larger group is more important.
    - Public self-awareness: anonymity means we won't face any judgement from others or punishment.

Institutional aggression in the context of prisons

- **The importation model: Irwin and Cresssey (1962)** argued that aggression is a result of individual differences, not being in a prison. This is due to the argument that prisoners will behave the same way inside the prison as they would outside the prison due to their disposition.
- **Disposition: DeLesi (2004)** researched a group of 813 juvenile offenders and found that certain dispositional traits, such as impulsivity, correlated to violent behaviour. When he compared his research group to a control group, he concluded that dispositional factors affect their chance of being violent.
- **Deprivation model: Clemmer (1958)** suggested that the intense deprivation inside prisons is a cause of aggressive behaviour. The lack of entertainment and the lack of ability to properly fulfil physiological needs all increase the risk of aggressive behaviour as it increases competition for resources.

Media influences on aggression

- **Computer games:**
  - **Bartholow and Anderson (2002)** compared levels of aggression whilst playing a violent video game (Mortal Combat) compared to playing a golf simulator. He found that those in the violent conditions delivered sounds of a greater decibel by 1.3.
  - **DeLesi (2013)** found a strong correlation between amount of time spent playing violent video games and those in a juvenile detention centre.
  - **Anderson (2010)** conducted a meta-analysis of 136 studies to show a strong correlation between exposure to aggressive media and increased chance of observers becoming aggressive in both collectivist and individualist cultures.
- **Desensitisation, disinhibition and cognitive priming:**
  - **Desensitisation:** when a person is repeatedly exposed to violent acts, it causes them to regard it as more normal and therefore feel less empathy for the victim. For example, **Weisz and Earls (1995)** found that men who had watched a film with a violent rape scene in it were more accepting of the assertion that women often make false accusations and were less likely to find a defendant guilty in a rape trial.
  - **Disinhibition:** occurs through the process of social learning where our restrains towards violence are lowered through social learning. The media can be seen to reward aggressive behaviour and show minimal negative consequence. This leads to new social norms being developed.
  - **Cognitive priming: Huesmann (1988)** theorised that repeated exposure to violent acts being rewarded results in us developing a mental framework which allows us to make predictions about violent behaviour in real life scenarios. This changes our cognition and we are primed to anticipate consequences of aggression.

Defining and measuring crime

- Crime is an illegal act that can be punished by incarceration or other punishments after a legal trial.
- **Historical issues:** what was considered a crime at one point in history may not be a crime in modern society e.g. homosexuality.
- **Cultural issues:** some 'crimes' aren't considered 'crimes' in different cultures. For example, in one culture, hitting a child may be seen as a form of 'tough love', but in the UK, smacking a child is considered punishable by law according to the 2004 Child's Protection Act.

Offender profiling

- **The typology approach:**
  - This uses a pre-established typology to place offender in two categories: organised or disorganised offenders.
  - **Organised offenders:** socially and sexually competent individuals who plan ahead of their crimes and are very unlikely to leave any evidence or clues at the crime scene. They have a 'type' of victim (e.g. Jeffery Dahmer targeted young men and boys). They carry out their crime in a precise and deliberate manner.
  - **Disorganised offenders:** socially and sexually incompetent individuals who commit spontaneous crimes. They are more likely to leave clues at the crime scene due to a lack of planning. Their attacks don't seem to be premeditated with no specific target.
  - **Offender profiling:** using these categories, police can reduce a list of suspects and create a smaller field of investigation.
- **Data driven approach:** doesn't use pre-establish typology, instead drawing from the crime scene and eyewitness testimony. This approach includes investigative psychology and geographical profiling.
  - **Investigative psychology:** process where a crime is recorded onto a database. New evidence is then matched in the database in order to create a hypothesis about the likely motivations, social demographic, and likely characteristics of the offender. This emphasises the importance of time and place and the idea of **interpersonal coherence,** which is the theory that the way the offender treats the victim as a reflection of how they feel in their own life.
  - **Geographical profiling:** every offender has a base where they operate from. This can be identified through mapping previous crimes, usually forming a circle with the base at the centre, which can then be used to predict and prevent further crimes.

Biological explanations of offending behaviour

- Biological explanations focus on the role of heritability and candidate genes in criminal behaviour.
- **Christiansen (1977)** found concordance rates of 33% for MZ twins and 12% for DZ twins. This shows there is a moderate genetic link between criminal behaviour and heritability.
- Candidate genes: **Tilhonen (2014)** researched abnormalities in the MAOA gene and CDH-13 gene. They both code for neurotransmitters and are linked with the development of ADHD. It increases the likelihood of being a criminal by a vast amount.
- Neural explanations: focus on those with antisocial personality disorder. It's very commonly found amongst criminals. **Raine (1997)** found that criminals have a lower activity level in their prefrontal cortex which is responsible for logical thought and decision making.
- **Keysers (2013)** found that criminals effectively have a 'neural switch' which allows them to turn empathy on or off, which explains why some criminals lack remorse and guilt for their victims.

Dealing with offending behaviour

- **Custodial sentencing:** the aims of custody are deterrence, incapacitation, retribution, and rehabilitation. However, the effects of this sentencing are generally negative. These include stress, depression, and institutionalisation. Institutionalisation is a big problem as prison life is extremely boring and the same day-to-day, leading to high reoffending rates and a lack of rehabilitation.
- **Behaviour modification in custody:** token economies based on operant conditioning – in custody, selected socially-acceptable behaviours may be rewarded with tokens (a secondary reinforcer) that can be exchanged for a privilege (the primary reinforcer). **Hobbs and Holt (1976)** studied 125 male juveniles in an industrial school and found that using token economies caused a significant increase in desirable behaviour from the majority of boys.
- **Anger management:** **Novaco (1997)** found that anger management focuses on identifying and dealing with emotion that come before anger, not preventing anger in the first place. This is an 'eclectic' approach as offenders are taught skills from a variety of different approaches. There are three stages:
  - **Cognitive preparation:** offenders identify patterns of emotion that occur during, after and before aggression which helps them to predict their anger.
  - **Skills acquisition:** the offender learns techniques that can be used to manage their anger (e.g. breathing techniques to regulate their mood and emotions). This is direct learning where the therapist does the technique and the offender copies them.
  - **Application practice:** offender applies learnt skills to a real life situation that would make them angry. If there are successful, the therapist positively reinforced them.
- **Restorative justice:**
  - **Braithwaite (2002)** found that restorative justice programmes use a different perspective than other methods. This approach aims to focus on the victim, and how they were affected by the aggressive behaviour. There are mediated conversations between the victim and the offender outside of the courtroom.
  - The restorative justice council create guidelines for what survivors, offenders, and mediators can do. If an offender wants to, they can pay for damages caused to the victim, apologise, and show remorse for their actions.

Psychological explanation of offending behaviour

- **Criminal personality theory:**
  - **Eysenck (1964)** proposed that criminal behaviour is linked to personality, which can be measured along three dimensions:
    - Extraversion–Introversion (level of cortical arousal)
    - Neuroticism–Stability (emotional stability and response to stress)
    - Psychoticism (added later, linked to aggression, hostility, and lack of empathy)
  - The criminal personality is typically high in neuroticism and extraversion, and also high in psychoticism.
  - Biological basis: personality traits are influenced by the activity of the nervous system (e.g. arousal levels, sensitivity to stress). These biological factors affect how individuals respond to conditioning and socialisation.
  - People with the criminal personality are less responsive to socialisation processes. They do not learn to associate antisocial behaviour with punishment effectively. This makes them more likely to engage in crime, as they fail to view antisocial behaviour as negative.
- **Cognitive distortions:**
  - **Kohlberg (1958)** put forth **three universal laws of moral reasoning:**
    - **Pre-conventional level:** avoiding punishment or self-interest.
    - **Conventional level:** 'good boy attitude,' acting in accordance with social expectations and laws.
    - **Post-conventional level:** social contracts and universal ethical principles to justify responses.
  - He theorised that criminals have an immature sense of reasoning. They act at the pre-conventional level whereas non-criminals operate on the conventional or post-conventional level, giving them empathy and more socially acceptable behaviour.
  - Cognitive distortions are examples of dysfunctional thought processing that show errors in logic. The two main cognitive distortions are:
    - **Hostile attribution bias (HAB):** when individuals view non-threatening situations as hostile, so hostility is their immediate reaction.
    - **Minimalisation:** common amongst sex offenders; used to cope with any feelings of guilt or regret where they will downplay the significance of their crimes and the effect on their victim.
- **Differential association theory:**
  - **Sutherland (1939)** suggested that crime is a learned behaviour and can be explained by social leaning theory. Role models are criminal peers that they admire and strive to be like so act accordingly. It's possible to predict the likelihood of someone to become a criminal based on exposure to pro-criminal attitudes.
  - Individuals will learn attitudes towards crime as well as how to accomplish the crimes. If they are exposed to more pro-criminal attitudes than anti-criminal attitudes, there is a high likelihood of them becoming criminal.

Describing addiction

Defining addiction is complex but needs to include the following characteristics:

- **Withdrawal symptoms:** occur when a patient stops taking the substance they are addicted to, or take a smaller dose. These are very unpleasant experiences and they cause symptoms such as insomnia and nausea. This only encourages addicts to keep taking the substance as they do not want to experience withdrawal.
- **Tolerance:** this is where a higher dosage of a drug no longer produces a desired result for a patient. This results in a spiral of usage when large doses are required. This can cause major problems in surgery where drug addicts need much higher doses of anaesthetic due to their tolerance against sleep inducing drugs.
- **Physical dependence:** well withdrawal symptoms subside when a drug has been administered to a patient. It shows that their body cannot function normally without having the drug in their body which causes physiological changes. This is different to psychological dependence which occurs when patients experience the need to acquire the drugs in order to experience the pleasurable effects. This leads to the development of a habit.

Risk factors in development of addiction

- **Genetic factors:**
  - Individuals can inherit candidate genes which provide them with a hereditary predisposition towards developing an addiction.
  - A biological susceptibility mechanism has been shown to be low levels of D2 receptors in the brain. This means that fewer dopamine molecules combine to the receptors and initiate action potentials in the postsynaptic membrane.
  - Abnormal gene expression of the gene coding for the CYP2A6 enzyme – low levels of this enzyme leads to slower rates of nicotine breakdown. This reduces the concentration of nicotine metabolites within the brain synapses, which decreases the likelihood of developing a nicotine addiction.
- **Personality:** impulsivity and anti-social personality disorder and linked to an increased risk of developing an addiction. Impulsivity is linked to having little thought about the outcome of risk-taking behaviours.
- **Social and environmental influences:**
  - Family influences: links to how closely monitored children are by their parents as well as how often they see their parents using substances. The higher the exposure to these substances, the more likely a child is to also get addicted.
  - Friends: have more of an influence on the development of addictions compared to family influences. Friends create norms surrounding taking addictive substances and provide more access and availability to get these substances than family.
  - Stress: chronic stress is not a direct trigger for addiction, but when paired with an environmental stressor, it is more likely to result in addiction.

Explanations for nicotine addiction

- **Brain neurochemistry:**
  - **Dani and Heinemann's (1996)** desensitisation hypothesis theorised that there was an antagonistic effect between acetylcholine and dopamine, especially in areas of the brain that control feelings of pain and pleasure.
  - Nicotinic receptors allow acetylcholine and nicotine to bind to them. An action potential is generated and therefore the acetylcholine is broken down. However, due to the nicotine being there, the receptors go through desensitisation which is where they become less sensitive and therefore leads to feelings of heightened pleasure.
  - This process leads to dopamine being released in the mesolimbic system, which interacts with nicotinic receptors that provide feelings of heightened pleasure
  - When there is a lack of nicotine, the receptors become hypersensitive to acetylcholine again, which can result in feelings of high anxiety and nausea.
  - Gradually, the concentration of nicotine needed to provoke deregulation increases, so a tolerance to nicotine is developed.
- **Social learning theory:**
  - Psychologists argue that nicotine addictions can be explained by using social learning theory as it is a learned behaviour that can be acquired through classical or operant conditioning.
  - Positive reinforcement suggests that we carry out certain behaviours because we're motivated by the rewards. Smoking can be positively reinforced by the reward of positive feelings and heightened pleasure. Therefore, we want to smoke again to get the same rewards of feeling good.
  - Negative reinforcement suggest we carry out certain behaviours because we want to avoid unpleasant consequences. People continue to smoke as they don't want to experience the unpleasant consequences of withdrawal symptoms.
  - Cue reactivity suggests there are certain environmental cues which increased likelihood of doing the addictive behaviour (e.g. smoking at a social gathering). These environments contain primary reinforces and secondary reinforces. These reinforces work together to reinforce and maintain excessive smoking habits and nicotine addiction.

Explanations for gambling addiction

- **Social learning theory:**
  - This addiction links to cue reactivity and five types of reinforcement: positive, negative, variable, partial, and vicarious.
  - There are many cues which continuously leads sufferers of gambling addictions to further increase the addiction. For example, slot machines in pubs or the presence of lottery machines in shops act as secondary enforces because they are associated with the addictive feelings of gambling.
  - Partial reinforcement is the idea that behaviours that are most hard to stop are not produced through consistent rewarding of desirable behaviours. When gamblers win, it is unlikely to happen frequently. This way they're more likely to gamble more to chase the short term high of an uncommon win. This motivates them to continue trying until they win again.
  - Variable reinforcement is based on the idea that a gambler only has a certain statistical chance of winning. They're motivated by the constant temptation and statistical justification to keep playing. In their mind the more they play the more statistically likely they are to win.
  - Positive reinforcement maintains gambling by rewarding gamblers for their successful bets. They will get praise from others, a thrill. When other gamblers see other gamblers win, they are more likely to continue gambling themselves. This is an example of vicarious reinforcement as they want to achieve the same rewards as the winners.
  - Negative reinforcement is carried out by providing the gambler with an escape from their daily struggle. It's a short term shift of focus to better feeling.
- **Cognitive theory:**
  - Cognitive biases play important role in distorted views of expectancy. There are four key types of cognitive biases:
    - **Faulty perceptions** e.g. thinking the loses cannot continue forever
    - **Selective recall** e.g. only remembering the rewards
    - **Skills and judgements:** e.g. the illusion of control or thinking you can stop anytime
    - **Personal traits:** e.g. believing in luck or superstitions
  - **Irrational idea of expectancy:** the benefits of gambling must exceed the costs, further explaining why people focus on the perceived positives of their addiction and ignores the real losses.